LIFE STO.
LEGENDARY ENTERTAINER

[ELIZABETH RAMSEY]

QUEEN OF PHILIPPINE

ROCK n' ROLL

Sansu Ramsey

RSJ Production
Publisher

Elizabeth Ramsey, Queen of Philippine Rock N' Roll
Copyright @ 2017 by RSJ Production

All rights reserved.
No part of this book may be reproduced in any form or by any means without the written permission of the copyright owner and the publisher.

Published and exclusively distributed by:
RSJ Production
To order the Special Edition copies, email:
Srblackcherry1@gmail.com

Book design by: Sansu Ramsey/Dennis Wadlington/Edwin Lozada
Translated by: Malou Rivera/Sansu Ramsey
Edited by: Sansu Ramsey/Dennis Wadlington/Lorna Deitz/Cherrieh Pittman

ISBN-10: 1975919726
ISBN-13: 978-1975919726

WARNING:

THIS BOOK CONTAINS SCENES OF EXTREME VIOLENCE AND ADULT LANGUAGE THAT IS NOT SUITABLE AND SHOULD NOT BE READ AND VIEWED BY CHILDREN 13 YEARS OLD AND BELOW.

DEDICATION

This book is dedicated to the fans, family, and friends of Ms. Elizabeth Ramsey, who gave her their love and support when she was with us. She now rests in peace with God.

DISCLAIMER

A memoir is what you want it to be. This is a work of creative non-fiction based on Ms. Elizabeth Ramsey's digital audio recordings for more than five years. Sansu Ramsey, the author, was asked by her mother, Elizabeth, to digitally tape her stories, to write about her struggles, including the "miracles" that enabled Elizabeth to rise above pitfalls and adversities that threatened to pull her down. The events are portrayed to the best of Elizabeth Ramsey's recollections.

While all the stories in this book are true, it may not be entirely factual. Details of some narratives were fictionalized including dialogue, the characters, and their personality traits, locations, with some of the names altered and invented for literary effect. Although the contents of the book are not written to represent word-for-word transcripts or details, Ms. Ramsey's book is a combination of key facts and certain embellishments. Witnesses to certain incidents have died. Important court documents that Ms. Ramsey mentions in her recollections have disappeared forever because the city hall of San Carlos City was burned down. Sansu Ramsey, the author, altered her mother's narrative by translating her Visayan/Tagalog languages into the universal English language for clarity and readability.

CONTENTS

Acknowledgment	6
Preface	7
Introduction	9
Early Years	10
Growing Pains	32
Mysterious Encounters	43
Adulthood	47
Life Being Married	52
Adventures	62
Dreams Do Come True	68
Success	70
Faith	79
Stardom & Accomplishments	93
Funny Hour	104
Memorable Moments	108
A True Testimony About Her Faith	119
Grief of Her Passing	122
Eulogy	134

ACKNOWLEDGMENT

My heartfelt gratitude goes to Dennis Wadlington, the love of my life, for his empathetic collaboration, inspiration, and motivation in the writing and copyediting of this book.

My deepest appreciation to the following friends who collaborated with me: Malou Rivera, Edwin Lozada, and Lorna Lardizabal Dietz and Jennifer Lindsay (Co-Editor).

Special thanks to the following: my loving children, Dyana Ware and Rodney Ware, for their encouragement and guidance; Mary Ann Pittman, my older sister and her daughter, Cherrieh Pittman, for their support when I needed them the most; to all the family members who helped researched pictures and provided information for the contents of this book.

It also goes without saying that I am very grateful to the Santo Niño Group in the Philippines led by Rose and Johnny Uy, Gina and Sam Tria, and the government officials of San Carlos City, Negros Occidental.

A special recognition is bestowed to our family and friends for their support and love, the congregation and pastors at St. James the Apostle, Our Lady of Peace and St. Edwards, California and to those who shared memorable moments with my mama.

PREFACE

As the third child of the legendary Philippines' Queen of Rock 'N Roll, I felt honored and compelled to share Elizabeth's life story with you and the rest of the world because she touched us as an outstanding and excellent singer as well as that of an extraordinary comedian, actress, and a lifelong humanitarian. No one can ever doubt the existence of Ms. Elizabeth Ramsey in the Philippines' entertainment industry. To her, being a dark brown-skinned Filipina was not a hindrance but a symbol of the Philippines' cultural history and diversity. She broke all the color barriers in the Philippine entertainment world. Elizabeth was the first Filipina of Jamaican and Spanish descent who was in a class of her own in stage and theater, radio, movies, and television. In spite of her positive, influential person, it was always her selfless attitude and compassion that drove her to care not only for her family but also for those in need of affection, in kindness and financial support.

Elizabeth Ramsey was known for having the uncanny ability of a "third eye", i.e. she could predict someone's past and future by simply looking at the person. Ma always found time to share inspirational, funny, and scary stories with people.

My mother, Elizabeth, was a devout Catholic, never lacking in kindness and concern toward family and friends. From sunrise to sunset, you could always hear her words of encouragement, **"No worry! Everything will be fine. Santo Niño will take care of your problems!"**

One day, a month before her passing, Ma told me privately that she had a very strong feeling that it was time to finish the digital audio recording she had started more than five years ago. It was as if my mother had a premonition that she would soon leave us. She finished her recordings within two weeks. Ever since I was a young girl, Ma would repeat the same words to me: "I want you to write and publish my book so everyone will know more about me --- and remember me." My mother, Elizabeth Ramsey, did not want to simply disappear from her family, fans, and friends although she felt she had to prepare herself when Santo Niño called her to rest.

The Visayan language version of her life story has been translated into English in this book, **"Elizabeth Ramsey, Queen of Philippine Rock N' Roll"**, for everyone to understand and be a part of her amazing adventures.

Ma, now that you have gone home, I want you to know that we fulfilled your wishes. You will always be one of the Philippines' most legendary entertainers, forever our treasure:

"ELIZABETH RAMSEY,
THE QUEEN"

INTRODUCTION

These are the earliest recollections of my life which will include the discovery of my family history and generation that follows. Before you start reading my book, just always remember that I carried these memories all my life and trusted my dear daughter Sansu to write the way I wanted it to be. It is a shame that I am no longer with you to hear your "Oohs!" "Aahs!" "What!" "Really!" "Who!" "For Real!" But you know what! I am now with my dearest Santo Niño watching over all of you reading my book and eating rice with stinky fish. I hope you will be inspired, have learned from my mistakes, motivated, know the importance of family, faith, and love. I apologize in advance to anyone that I may have offended because the truth hurts but needs to be told.

Okay now, everyone! This is now where I pass the baton to my daughter Sansu to begin telling you how my memoir started.

THE EARLY YEARS

The Philippine-American War was a conflict between the United States and the First Philippine Republic from 1899-1902 when the Philippine Government at that time accepted the Americans to organize a deal between the two countries. During and after the war, there were United States Merchant Marines stationed in Mactan Island, Cebu.

According to my mother, Elizabeth, the story begins from the roots of the Ramsey family, my grandfather, the father of my mother, **Mr. Arthur "Arturo" Ramsey.** Jamaican family descendant originally from the Kingston, Jamaica. He was proud to enlist in the U.S. Merchant Marine to serve in ways as an obligation to your country is also part of serving humanity. He was appointed in service during the conflict of the Philippine-American-War, where he was stationed in Mactan Island, Philippines. He fell in love with the Philippine Islands so much that he started to explore Mactan Islands. He did an intensive geographical study of the neighboring islands around Cebu. He intended to stay in the Philippines for the rest of his life. He wanted to make sure that he could navigate from Cebu to whatever island he chose when the time came for him to jump ship. After all his careful geographical study, he found a small beautiful neighboring city in the province of Negros

Occidental named San Carlos City. The city is located at the crossroads of four major cities in the Visayas: Cebu City, Bacolod City, Iloilo City and Dumaguete City. In the year of 1912, during the first years of the American occupation, the social climate of the people in the city of San Carlos was gauged by its sugar cane industry which greatly enhanced the economic life of the people. Mr. Ramsey was a well-skilled shipping cargo engineer. In the latter part of 1915, the life story of Grandpa Ramsey began in the city of San Carlos. After a long time, contemplating, he finally gained enough courage to jump ship. He kept going and never looked back. Once he reached the pier, he then paid for a boat ride from Mactan, Cebu City to Bacolod City, then he took a bus ride going to San Carlos City. He went UA (unauthorized absence) from the United States Merchant Marine base shipyard. According to Wikipedia, in military terminology, desertion is the abandonment of a duty or post without permission and is done with the intention of not returning. This is in contrast to "Unauthorized Absence (UA)" or "Absence Without Leave (AWOL)" which refers to a temporary absence. The use of "UA" by the Navy/Marine Corps and "AWOL" by the Army/Air Force has a historical component. Prior to the enactment of the Uniform Code of Military Justice in 1951, the services were governed by separate laws. However, its official title under the current Uniform Code of Military Justice (UCMJ) is "AWOL." It simply means not being where you are supposed to be at the time you are supposed to be there. After he left the shipyard, the military now considered him either missing in action or a deserter. If he was caught, he would be court-martialed (i.e.), a judicial court determines the guilt of members of the armed forces, subject to military law, and if the defendant is found guilty, to decide upon punishment. – according to "Wikipedia").

He went UA for a year where he hid in San Carlos City while renting a room from a local family until the military stopped searching for him. He survived on a small portion of the money that he had saved. When the smoke cleared from military search, he then started looking for a job around the city. His landlord informed him that the Central Milling Company in San Carlos City was looking for someone who could operate the sugar cane hand mill. A sugar cane hand mill is a piece of equipment that crushes the sticks of sugar cane to extract the juice. The sugar cane juice is then processed into molasses which ultimately gives us brown sugar. He practically dressed himself up and headed toward the Central Milling Company to apply for the position. This was his last chance to survive in the city because his savings had depleted tremendously. He was so nervous and paranoid because he wasn't sure if he was qualified for the job since he was not a Filipino citizen. In the back of his mind, he was also worried that US Marine is still looking for him. He presented himself as a prestigious intellectual, well-traveled applicant.

A week later, the Central Milling Company's Human Resources office notified him that he was accepted for the position as the chief engineer for a Molino (hand mill). He was extremely surprised that he got one of the most dignified positions in the company. He became the sole operator of the sugar cane hand mill. His prestigious position with the company and his charming personality made him a well-respected employee by other associates as well as the entire community. Since the city was so small, everyone knew each other well including but not limited to their personal affairs. After several months passed, he was now able to afford to purchase his own house. Besides being the chief engineer of the sugar hand mill, he was also employed as a foreman and the railroad track engineer. He was the overall operations supervisor of all railroad track workers who were responsible for building the railroad tracks that ran through San Carlos City, Negros Occidental to Makapso, Negros Oriental. The railroad tracks were the only means to transport sugar cane.

Grandpa Arturo Ramsey was very smart, stern had an authoritarian leadership style, and he behaved like a true gentleman. His family migrated originally from Jamaica, and he was raised speaking with a very eloquent British accent. As noted in history, Jamaica was under the colonial rule of Britain since the year of 1655. His skin color was charcoal black and he stood approximately 5'5" tall. He was a very strong-minded private man whom you rarely saw smiling. In the year of 1917, after the First World War, the planter industry of San Carlos City dramatically increased their sugar producing crops, greatly improving their economy which was attributed to Grandpa Ramsey's excellent analytical and managerial skills.

My smooth Grandpa Ramsey started socializing and eventually met a beautiful charming woman at one of the city's local gatherings. Each time their paths crossed, he began to flirt with her even though he knew that she was a married woman. Their friendship and mutual attraction grew and became a sexual love affair. After months of blistering physical attractions with each other, she became pregnant. She was perplexed at how she was going to tell her family and most of all how she was going to explain this mess to her husband. She eventually had to inform Grandpa Ramsey that she was carrying his baby. Then she asked him, "How are we going to handle this situation?"

Of this unexpected situation, Grandpa Ramsey told his pregnant woman friend that he would bear no responsibility for the predicament. She was so distraught by his nonchalant response to her condition, which left her with no choice but to inform her family. Unfortunately, her family had turned their backs on her to the extent that she ended up giving birth to their child alone. The child closely resembled my grandpa so much that she named him Arturo Jr. This charming woman already had four other children from her marriage. Her relationship with my grandfather was doomed from the start. It was not surprising that their sexual passion and desire did not flourish after she gave birth to Arturo Jr. She wanted to remain married and tried to reconcile with her husband. Sadly, the husband could not forgive her infidelity and decided to end their marriage. My grandfather wanted no part of having any relationship with anyone because he wished to remain single and continue playing the field. Therefore, she was left all alone to raise Arturo Jr. with her other four children.

One afternoon, on the way home, through a heavily wooded roadside, he stumbled upon a beautiful fair skinned young Filipina/Spanish girl taking a bath in the secluded neighborhood *"sapa"* (brook- a natural stream of water smaller than a river). Her beauty was so mesmerizing that he compared her to a *"dewata"* (fairy). Standing in hiding in the bushes, he watched and enjoyed the sight of the beautiful long, black haired innocent girl splashing the water all over her body. This unguarded young girl was enjoying the stillness of the breeze and the rays of the sun softening the quietness of the surroundings. He watched her until she finished bathing, dressed herself up, then proceeded to walk away and disappear into the woods. He was left shocked and in disbelief at the beauty that he just witnessed. He went home feeling dazed and kept thinking and wondering when he could see her again. Days and weeks passed by, but he never saw her again at the secluded brook. For weeks, he was never able to get the thought of her off his mind; he started inquiring from his co-workers about this beautiful young girl whom he saw from the brook. Who was she? Where was she from? He then described to his co-workers what he had seen was the most captivating, attractive young girl taking a bath in the secluded neighboring brook. He had never seen the likes of such beauty in the entire time he had spent in San Carlos City. Everyone told him that he was going crazy because no one had ever gone to that very secluded brook. Because of his determination to find her, he vigorously never stopped inquiring about her to his co-workers and to anyone he encountered. As a long period of time passed by, he continued to ask the whereabouts of the young girl to almost every one of his colleagues, friends, neighbors and even strangers off the streets. Coincidently, one of his co-workers finally recognized who he was referring to. Turns out, this fellow happened to be the young girl's uncle. After this revelation, he was finally vindicated, proving to everyone that he was not crazy after all and that he had seen the most beautiful young girl at the secluded brook. His reputation was restored and he became the happiest man in town. Now, every time he went home, he always took the longest route so that he could walk around the brook and hope to catch a glimpse of that mysterious, beautiful girl again that caused such a stir in his mind, distracted his focus and concentration at his workplace. The said uncle/co-worker eventually offered my grandfather the information on the girl's name and where she was from. Her uncle agreed to what Grandpa Ramsey's description of her niece looks, like a "fairy". He was absolutely correct, that she was a stunning image of an exuberant beauty, embedded with astonishing fair soft white skin, accented with her high rosy cheeks and charming smile. On top of all her beautiful characteristics, she was a sweet, innocent and very soft-spoken shy girl. She was very private in her inner personal feelings that she only talked to her family and limited young friends.

Her name was Marcelina "Liling" Indino Rivera (Spanish/Filipina)

Every day, Grandpa Ramsey continued to take the same route through the heavily wooded area by the secluded brook. Finally, the moment arrived that this beautiful innocent young girl named Liling was back in the lake in her usual private moment enjoying the warm water and the calmness of the breeze. For years since she was a little girl, she and her parents had always visited the same spot. It was customary for her to take the bath quite often. From being a little girl till she reached her teenage year, no one has ever bothered her while she bathed in this far distant, private area of the brook. Out of nowhere, here comes Grandpa Ramsey walking towards her. For a young girl, this was the most frightening encounter to see; a charcoal skinned dark man looking at her while she was naked and totally vulnerable while trying to put her clothes back on. She stood still speechless because she did not know if this man was an Aeta (native black Filipino from the mountains). Aetas were also known for taking strangers to their villages. My grandfather startled her by addressing her name, "Liling!" She was now more frightened than ever by him calling her out by name. She was thinking about how she could get away from him while she was trying to put her clothes back on. This young minded girl struggled with what direction she should take to get away from him. She was only able to put on her panties but not her dress. While he was approaching her, he kept saying "Liling!" She was only able to speak in a soft, frightened voice, *"Kinsa ka? Nganong nahibalo ka sa akong ngalan?"* (Who are you? Why do you know my name?) Grandpa Ramsey replied, *"Ako mang gipango tana ang imong tiyo. Amigo man nako ang imong tiyo. Liling guapa kaayo ka."* (I asked your uncle. Your uncle is a friend of mine. Liling, you are so beautiful.) Grandpa Ramsey started getting closer and closer until he was in front of her but not quite close enough to grab her. Liling was shivering from the coldness of the breeze because the sun was starting to set. Liling, so naïve then speaking again, in her soft scared voice, *"Nong, ayaw lang intawon ug duol kay mulakaw naman ko."* (Sir, please do not come closer because I'm leaving.) As soon as she said that, Grandpa Ramsey started charging her. She grabbed her dress and started to run as fast as she could. He chased her through the woods until he eventually caught up with her. He was able to grab her arm which caused her to fall down to the ground. Liling then said in her shivering, petrified voice, *"Nong, ayaw intawon kog sakti!"* (Sir, please do not hurt me!) The more she begged him not to hurt her, the more aggressive he became. He now had full control over her helpless body while she kept kicking and pushing him away from her. He was playing her anxiety by trying to convince Liling to stop fighting him so he would leave her alone. Liling was so naïve that she started listening to him and stopped fighting him. She now started to put her guard down. As soon as she felt a bit calmer, he then proceeded with his attack. He tore off her underwear and unzipped his pants, put his hand over her mouth and abused her while she was gasping and screaming for help.

Liling was so helpless, unable to move, out of breath, prevented from screaming, exhausted from her attempts at escape that all she can do was cry. Tragically, no one ever came to the rescue. When the ordeal was over, he told her not to tell anyone or he would harm her again. She watched him disappear into the woods. She was now in pain and bleeding from losing her virginity. She was left naked, crying, scared and felt so violated. For a thirteen-year-old girl, this was a traumatic incident that would never be forgotten. She got up, put her dress back on and walked gingerly towards her house. She continued to cry but she knew that she had to stop crying before she got home. She had to remember what Grandpa Ramsey previously warned her, that there would be consequences if she told anyone what happened in the woods and that he will hurt her again.

Months passed by, and Liling never said anything to her parents about what happened in the woods and she never went back to the brook again. After that malicious encounter with my grandfather, Liling still felt so violated and in shock but unable to express herself to anyone the horrible pain that she experienced. She started vomiting uncontrollably and felt dizzy all the time. Her mother started noticing that her belly was getting bigger. While she was lying in her bed, her mother sat beside her and started to ask, *"Dai, ngano man nga ang imong tiyan gadako unya ga si ka pud ug gasakit?"* (Girl, why is it that your belly is growing and you are always sick?) She then went into a fetal position and started to cry. Sobbingly, she confessed that there was a very dark black man in the woods who raped her. Her mother's face was so paled from being shocked, she did not know what to say. Her mother then gave her a big comforting hug to calm her down and gave her assurance that she and her father will find him. After she fell asleep from crying, her mother then went straight to the living room to tell her husband. Liling's father was so furious that he was ready to take action that same night. He then realized that it was too late to confront Mr. Ramsey at his workplace. They knew that it was not hard to identify the dark-skinned man in San Carlos City because my Grandpa Ramsey was the only one that fits that description.

On the following day, Liling's parents woke up early, ready to face Mr. Ramsey. Liling's mother, in her enraged state, told her husband, "*Adtu nang itum na inatay!*" (Get that black devil!). Liling's father then proceeded quickly with determination to confront him. As soon as he arrived at Central Milling Company, he went straight to my grandfather Ramsey's office. Liling's father did not wait for my Grandpa Ramsey to come back to his office, instead, he went marching into the location where grandfather was. As soon as Liling's father saw my Grandpa Ramsey, he launched towards him. But when the co-workers saw that he was ready to throw a punch at my grandfather, they tackled him. He then started yelling, "*Negro! Patyon ti ka! Banyaga ka! Patyon ti ka!*" (Black man! I will kill you! You have no shame! I will kill you!). He kept repeating himself while the men were holding him back. Grandpa Ramsey then told everyone to leave them alone and told Liling's father to calm down so they could talk privately. Liling's father then promised to settle down so that they can have a reasonable conversation. My grandfather then took Liling's father to a very private area where they could have a civil conversation. Grandpa Ramsey, without hesitation, started the conversation by expressing his sincere apology for what he had done and begged for his forgiveness. He had no way of knowing how to undo the vicious action he committed. He was remorseful and ashamed of what he did to Liling. He did not know how to extend his earnest apology to Liling and to her parents. Liling's father then told him the surprising news that Liling looked like she was pregnant. He wanted Grandpa Ramsey to do the right thing and take full responsibility including letting Liling move into his home and marry her once she reached the age of 21 or suffer the consequences of being arrested and going to jail charged as a rapist. Since Grandpa Ramsey held a powerful position and did not want to tarnish his name, he negotiated with Liling's father. He had no choice but to say, "Yes, Sir!" that he would take the responsibility for his action by agreeing for Liling to live with him and to prepare for marriage when she turned 21 years of age. Liling's father, with no hesitation, expressed his contentment to their agreement and left pleased with the final outcome of their civil encounter.

After Liling's parent's last encounter with my Grandpa Ramsey, they proceeded to informed their daughter, Liling, of the verbal agreement details made with Grandpa Ramsey. It was the best arrangement they could all agree upon under the circumstances. As months passed by, Liling innocently asked her parents why her belly was growing, she always felt sick, and constantly looked for something to eat in weird hours of the day. Her parents then told her that she was carrying a baby which resulted from that unwanted vicious act of Mr. Ramsey. Liling was surprised and confused because she did not understand why a girl carried a baby in her belly, and for what did happen for her to be pregnant. Innocently, Liling's parents never taught her about the birds and bees story. By this time, Liling was in her second trimester, and definitely in need of more parental guidance. It would be a very careless decision on their part if they hand her over now to Grandpa Ramsey because he was so focused on his job that he would not have time to care for her. She would be left alone with no maternal guidance and medical care. Eventually, Liling's parents decided to wait for her to deliver the baby before surrendering her into the hands of Grandpa Ramsey. On May 9, 1930, Liling gave birth to a very healthy, handsome baby boy named:

Federico Ramsey (aka Peding).

Now my beautiful Grandma Liling recovered from the delivery of her baby boy, her parents were now ready to accompany her to Grandpa Ramsey's house to fulfill what was agreed upon by both parties. My Grandpa Ramsey had now welcomed them into his home. He was extremely delighted to hold the little baby boy for the very first time in his arms. Grandma Liling was still scared of him even though he was already a changed man.

    Many months passed by, Grandma Liling now lived with my grandfather, still fearful and so fragile to have any sexual relationship with him because of the vicious attack still lingering in her mind. Grandma Liling now had to be attentive to Grandpa Ramsey as a live-in girlfriend. At the age of fourteen years old, Grandma Liling was still very tender, and it was a learning process for her to be in a live-in relationship with someone you barely knew. She was focused more on raising their son, Peding. In reality, she was still a young girl at heart trying to learn about the relationships between a man and a woman. Sometimes, he would like to express his love to her but she just could not grasp the connections of a man hugging or giving a woman that emotional attention. Ultimately, he just couldn't resist his emotions towards Grandma Liling and he forced himself on her again. This was the only way he could get close to a woman that he was attracted to and learned to love. Because of Grandpa Ramsey's unwelcome sexual advances towards Grandma Liling, it resulted again in another pregnancy. This time she was pregnant with a beautiful healthy, baby girl named:

Elizabeth Ramsey (aka Beth)

My mother, Elizabeth was born on a blissful day on December 3, 1931. Grandpa Ramsey, as usual still could not contain his libido, so he kept having several acts of unprotected sexual affairs with other women. One of these women that he had a sexual affair with, bore him another baby boy named, Rudy. Yet another woman with whom he had several sexual relations with, also bore him another adorable baby girl named, Flora. Essentially, Grandma Liling was so tired of hearing talk from local gossip mongers about Grandpa Ramsey's constant affairs, and children with other women in the city and other neighboring cities, as well as being fed up with his unwanted sexual advances, she secretly began to pack her things and planned to move out with her children.

My strong-willed Grandma Liling's courage kicked in one day which gave her the momentum to pull herself out of this frustrating situation. Grandma Liling, emboldened to express her thoughts to Grandpa Ramsey, she said to him, *"Dag han na kaayo ka ug anak sa laeng babae. Gusto na nako mulakaw karon dayon ug dad-on nako ang atong mga anak. Tabangi lang ko ug bayad sa balay na akong balhinan. Para dili na ka mag huna-huna na pakaslan pa ko nimo."* (You have lots of kids from other women. I would like to leave now and take our children with me. Just help me pay the rent to the house that I'm moving into. You do not have to worry about marrying me.) Grandpa Ramsey was stone-faced and speechless but had no reason to hold her back. All he could do was watch her leave with their children because he knew she was telling the truth. After this incident, Grandpa Ramsey continued on having sexual relationships with other women and children from his various relationships. However, my grandfather did continue to financially support Grandma Liling and their children. Many months passed by, and meeting multiple women, he finally found the woman that he wanted to marry and they had a lasting relationship. Mrs. Ramsey bore two healthy children named, Henrietta and Alexander.

As goal-oriented woman, Grandma Liling continued to raise her children on her own with limited supplemental financial support from my Grandpa Ramsey. Unfortunately, the financial supplement was not enough to feed them and pay for their other household expenses. Grandma Liling had no education and never learned how to properly read and write. The only way for her and her children to survive was for her to work in the street carrying a basket on top of her head, full of fruits and vegetables for sale. From the early morning sunrise until nightfall, she walked around the city in her bare feet and only came home when she sold almost all of her fresh goods.

Wikipedia – sample picture of a Sari-clad woman in Mysore, India, balancing a basket of chikku (or sapota; a type of fruit) on her head like Grandma Liling did.

Grandma Liling got lucky sometimes in that she was able to sell all the food from her basket before night fell. Even during the rainy season, she continued to sell the fresh goods around the city while she was soaking wet and traveling with muddy feet. At times, she can only walk around wearing slippers because she did not have any shoes to wear.

When my Uncle Federico was three years old and my mother Elizabeth was two years of age, Grandpa Ramsey found out that the children were left alone unattended while Grandma Liling is out on the street all day selling fresh goods in order to make a living. When he found out where they lived, he inconspicuously visited the place. He saw the small, run down, little shack of a house where the living room, kitchen, the bedroom was all in one place. He felt so sorry for the living condition of his children and Grandma Liling. He kindly asked my grandmother's permission if he could have custody of the children when they grew a little older.

He would like to enroll them in a private Catholic school. He also extended his invitation to her that she would always be welcomed to visit them any day at his house whenever she pleased. Grandma Liling then looked at the faces of the children while trying to reason out if she should tell him to go away or accept his offer for the children's sake. After long and careful consideration, my Grandma Liling hesitantly made the decision to go ahead and hand over the custody of the children to Grandpa Ramsey. The children were so surprised and unwilling to go along with their father, that they started to cry intensely. With her back turned to her children, her head kept down, her face covered with her hands, while continually weeping she walked away. She did not have the audacity to see the anguished faces of her children as they disappeared from her sight.

My mother Elizabeth and uncle Peding are now living at the house of their father, Grandpa Ramsey with his current wife, their two biological children and Mrs. Ramsey's children from her previous relationships. Grandpa Ramsey did not waste his time in making advance arrangement to enroll my mother and my uncle at Santa Rita Catholic School. Grandpa Ramsey made sure that all his children will have the best education especially my mother Elizabeth because she was his favorite child. He was so fond of my mother Elizabeth's character as he knew that she had that special quality of very attentive to her surroundings, courageous and very smart.

After a year had passed by, my uncle Federico and my mother Elizabeth, began to miss their mother, Grandma Liling, so much that they decided to run away from the house of their father. They kept running and inquiring anyone they encountered in the city where they could find their mother, Liling. Lo' and behold, someone finally recognized the children and directed them to Grandma Liling's house. All of a sudden while Grandma Liling was out working doing her usual daily business of walking around the neighborhood selling fresh goods, something caught her eyes. She saw two black children running in front of her who seemed like they were lost and looking for their parents. She was completely surprised and recognized who these children were; she then joyfully screamed their names, *"Peding! Elizabeth! Na-a ko dinhi sa inyong likod! Hunong ug dagan!"* (Peding! Elizabeth! I'm behind you! Stop running!). Once they heard their names and recognized their mother's voice, they turned around and ran towards her. Grandma Liling quickly sat the basket of fresh goods down on the ground and hugged them tightly, *"Mga gihigugma kong anak! Daghang salamat sa pagbalik ninyo nako. Mahal ko kaayo mo! Sukad karon, dili na ko gustong ihatag mo sa inyong amahan!"* (My beloved children! Thank you so much for coming back to me. I love you so much! From now on, I will not give you back to your father!) After the reunion, she did not even bother to ask them why they were out in the street. It looked like they were running away from someone. She decided to keep the questions to herself and enjoyed the moment of their togetherness. She held their hands, cried extensively and went back to where her basket was, then headed back home.

    When Grandpa Ramsey found out that the children went back to my Grandma Liling's house, he immediately charged towards her home to take the children away from her. But this time Grandma Liling was ready to defend them. She stood in front of her house with a knife in her hand and said, *"Sige kuawa ning mga bata, kay patyon ka nako!"* (Go right ahead and take the kids, and I will kill you!). When Grandpa Ramsey realized she meant what she said, he then said, *"Oh sige! Dinha usa sila nimo, pero pag dako na nila, mag eskoyla sila sa Santa Rita."* (Okay! They will be with you for awhile but when they grow older, they are going to school at Santa Rita). From then on, Grandpa Ramsey left them alone, allowing the children to stay with my Grandma Liling for years.

My uncle Federico was so musically inclined, that he learned pretty quickly on how to play the guitar from an older gentleman. Since Federico loved to play the guitar, the older man who taught him different techniques on how to play the strings, surprised him with a guitar as a gift. Uncle Federico treasured his guitar so much that he played with it every chance he got. My mother Elizabeth, on the other hand, loved to sing and dance. One day, while my Uncle Federico and my mother Elizabeth were playing in front of their house with the other neighboring children, Grandma Liling stepped outside and yelled, *"Federico ug Elizabeth, adto mo didto sa tindahan kay nakulangan ko ug utan, ug kamatis sa akong giluto. Kuwaa ning diyes centimos!"* (Federico and Elizabeth, go to the store because I don't have enough vegetables and tomatoes for what I'm cooking. Take these 10 cents!). With no surprise, my mother was a very naughty high-spirited child; she grabbed the money from her mother's hand and off they went. Once they reached the store, my mother thought of an ingenious scheme to use the money to buy herself and Federico some snacks. My uncle Federico, the mellow kid he was, started to panic when he realized that they had used all the money. The smart one, my mother Elizabeth, being the mastermind of the situation thought of entertaining while begging for money. She was so lucky that uncle Federico always carried his guitar wherever he goes. She orchestrated how to beg by instructing my uncle Federico to play his guitar while she would be singing and dancing. Luckily, the people in the market enjoyed their live entertainment and start handing coins to my mother as a token of enjoyment. They succeeded with the trick that earned them money to buy the ingredients and remarkably some extra money that they set aside. The happy and excited little children felt that they had accomplished something. As soon as they got inside the house, my mother proudly told their mother on how they earned the extra money, *"Ma! Napalit namo ang utan ug kamatis. Nag palimus mi - maong ning daghan ang among kwarta. Ning kanta ko ug bayle unya si Peding ga tugtug sa iyahang gitara."* (Ma! We bought the vegetables and tomatoes. We begged - that's why we have lots of money. I sang and danced and Peding played his guitar.) Grandma Liling was so furious! She could hardly contain herself on how to explain to them the anger she felt in a nice way, *"Sus Ginoo! Mga anak ko! Ngano man gihimo ninyo na! Mahibaw-an gani ni Papa ninyo, kua-on na pud mo!"* (Oh my God! My children! Why did you do that! If your Papa finds out, he will take you back!) My uncle Federico then told my mother and said that it was her idea to beg for money because they had used it all for snacks. Grandma Liling went ahead and ordered the children to stay in the living room and wait there until she finished cooking dinner.

The neighborhood gossip mongers, who were not aware or had any knowledge about the children, never stopped talking about why Grandma Liling, such a beautiful Spanish/Filipina took care of dark complexioned children. My Grandma Liling was always glad and proud to walk with her children in the streets, hand-in-hand, in spite of the turning heads from the neighbors. When Grandma Liling, was young, she had never worn any shoes, because, during the Spanish colonial times, there were no larger shoe sizes to fit her feet. She was a tall, slimmer woman with large feet. Even during peacetime, she still had a hard time finding a pair of shoes that would fit her feet. At that time, only the United States and England were manufacturing imported larger shoe sizes for women in the Philippines. When the imported larger shoe sizes for women reached to the shore of San Carlos City, it became available at a central shoe store. She headed right away to the store to purchase her very first pair of shoes she ever owned. She treasured these pair of shoes so much that she only wore them on special occasions.

In order to support her children, Grandma Liling continued to sell food in the market and in the streets by carrying not just fruits but also a basket full of a variety of vegetables, and snacks. Unfortunately, the heavy lifting and constant walking on the rainy days or in over 100-degree heat sunny days without proper support in her feet, caused her to contract a very serious illness. She was so sick that she had to consult a doctor. She has then prescribed very expensive medication. In those days, my mother, and her brother Federico had no idea of what was going on with their mother and why she was so weak, losing a lot of weight and spitting blood. Eventually, she was not able to go out to sell food for a while because of the severity of her illness. She was so worried about how she could continue to raise her children with her health condition. Grandma Liling then had no choice but to go to Grandpa Ramsey's house and ask for his financial help. With her difficult circumstances, she begged my grandfather to give her some money so she could go to the drug store to buy her medication. She promised to repay him back once she recovered and got well enough to be able to resume selling food again. Grandpa Ramsey then agreed to give her money for her medications. My very frail Grandma Liling felt so relieved that she would be able to be treated and regain her health again. But my devious Grandpa Ramsey had something else in his mind on how she could repay her debt. Grandpa Ramsey with no surprise, before he gave his assistance the next day to my grandmother, he went to her house and requested to regain full custody of their children as part of the repayment agreement. Grandma Liling at this point had to make the most reasonable and practical decision for the sake of her children's living conditions. Without any other options and reservations, she had no choice but to agree to Grandpa Ramsey's conditions. With a heavy heart, Grandma Liling watched my mother Elizabeth (6 years old) and my uncle Federico (7 years old) was once again taken away from her by their father. Grandma Liling could hear the children crying, kicking and screaming, *"Mama! Dili mi gustong mo uban ni Papa. Mama, tabangi intawon mi!"* (Mama! We don't want to go with Papa. Mama, please help us!). Sobbing and crying, Grandma Liling had no choice but to keep silent. While her head was down, in a very soft sobbing voice, she said, *"Mga anak ko intawon, mahal na mahal ko kamo. Pasaylua ko sa akong sala na ibalik na pud nako kamo sa inyong amahan kay ayaw nako na mag antos mo na wala kamong makaon unya grabi kaayo ang akong sakit. Mag paka but an mo ha?! Ayaw intawon ug pa buyag! Kay dili mag dugay. Ma ayo ko ug mag uban tag usab."* (My children, I love you so much. I'm sorry that I have to hand you over to your father because I don't want you to suffer for not having food to eat and I'm also very sick. You better be good, okay?! Do not act up! It will not be that long. I will get better and we'll be together again).

My mother Elizabeth and my uncle Federico were so scared of their father that they stopped crying by the time they arrived at his house. Mrs. Ramsey was furious and dismayed that he brought the children back into their house. Grandpa Ramsey told his wife that from now on, they will be living with them (his wife, their two children together and his wife's children from previous relationships). She took their hands and squeezed them tight, whispered in their ears and said: *"Para dili mo mag dugay dinhi, akong himo on na mag antos mo adlaw adlaw"* (So that you do not live here long, I'm going to make sure you will suffer every day).

The next day, there was a knock at the door and there stood Arturo Jr. and his mother asking for Grandpa Ramsey to speak with him. She then told my grandfather that she is tired and had no more money to raise Arturo Jr. and her other four children without the support of her husband. Her husband was now willing to give her a second chance but with one condition, that she had to give up the custody of Arturo Jr. Her husband commanded her, *"Dili ko gusto na may Negro na bata ka sa atong balay, ihatag na siya sa iyang tinuod na amahan kung gusto nimong mag uban tag usab!"* (I don't like that there is a black child in our home, give him to his father if you want us to get back together again!) Without hesitation, she agreed to her husband's condition and that was why she was now at my Grandpa Ramsey's house to transfer the custody of little Arturo Jr. to his biological father. Even though this was a very difficult decision for a mother to make, she had no choice but to do what's best for all her children. This time, she was ready to settle down again with her husband, just like the good old days. Grandpa Ramsey then said, *"O Sige! Ihatag siya sa akong asawa ug lakaw na!"* (Okay! Give him to my wife and now, leave!) In a tearful and heart raging moment, she surrendered her responsibility in raising little Arturo Jr. She advised him to be good, and left him these assuring words, *"Dong! Mahal gyud ka nako! Pasaylua ko sa akong gihimo. Ayaw lang ug ka balaka, kay ako ka mang dungawon perme."* (Boy! I love you! Please forgive me for what I have done. Don't worry, I will visit you all the time.) She went on weeping while little Arturo Jr. cried uncontrollably when Mrs. Ramsey took him in the children's room.

GROWING PAINS

My mother, Elizabeth, at the age of six and my uncle, Federico, age seven, were now enrolled at Santa Rita Catholic School where most of the teachers predominantly were nuns. On the way home from school, my mother, and uncle, Federico had to walk alongside a Catholic Church. Inside the church, there was a huge statue of Jesus Christ crucified in the back of the pews where everyone always dedicated their petitions. My mother always asked her brother Federico to stop by the church on the way home because she needed to talk to a big crucifix and ask him something. Expressing curiosity, my mother then approached the crucifix and flicked the feet of Jesus Christ statue saying *"Huy! Tagai ku ug kwarta bi! Kay gigutum ko ug ang akong igsuon! I hulug lang diri sa akong kamut. Ug dili ka mang hatag ug kwarta, akong usab tusokon ang imong ti il"* (Hey! Give me money! My brother and me are hungry! Just drop the money in my hands. And if you don't give me money, I will flick your feet again). She stared at his feet waiting for something to drop but nothing happened while her brother, Federico was sitting in the pew praying and waiting for her to finish talking to the statue. The next day, she kept repeating her demands asking money and flicking his feet every time she saw Him. As days passed by, she got so frustrated, she started yelling at the statue, *"Nong! Unsa man! Dili ka man mang hatag ug kwarta! Kala in gud nimo uy! Sige na gud! Kay gigutum lagi ko ug ang akong igsuon - Sige na nong! maluoy ka! Bisag usa lang ka dako!"* (Sir! What's going on! You don't give me money! You are so mean! Come on now! Because my brother and I are very hungry – come on now Sir! Have mercy! Even only one cent!) One day on the way home, since she did not get her wish from Jesus Christ's statue, she saw this child who just bought his bananas on a stick from a guy selling bananas on the street. She quickly snatched the bananas from the kid's hand, punched him and ran as fast as she could. The child was so scared that he did not want to chase her and literally just cried out loud for help. At this point, my uncle, Federico was looking for his sister, Elizabeth but she was nowhere to be found. All of a sudden, here comes his sister holding freshly cooked bananas on a stick and out of breath. Uncle, Federico already knew that she did something wrong again. As a kid, my uncle Federico was a very good and honest little boy who always listened and followed every rule bestowed upon him. He always remembered what their mother, Liling, told him, *"Bantawi intawon ang imong igsuon kay maldita ra ba na siya kaayo! Gahi kayo siya ug ulo pero listo kaayo kay utokan man!"* (Please keep an eye on your sister because she is very naughty! She's hard headed but very energetic and very smart!) He was going crazy looking all over for his sister. After my uncle finally found his sister, he cautiously asked her where she had been. My uncle, Federico, reluctantly asked, *"Kinsa man ag naghatag nimo ug kwarta para ka makapalit ug saging?"* (Who gave you the money so you can buy the bananas?) His smarty-pants sister replied, *"Gihatag ra man ni atong taong nagbaligya ug saging kay na luoy man siya nako. Akong nawong kuno murag gutom kaayo!"* (The man that was selling the bananas gave it to me. He felt sorry for me because my face looked so hungry!). Of course, my uncle Federico did not believe her explanation. So, he persisted by telling her, *"Sige na day! E uli intawon ang saging sa tag iya, para dili masuko nato ang Ginoo. Bul ugon unya ka pag na hibaw an gani ni Papa Arturo"* (Come on now girl! Please return the bananas to its owner so that God will not get mad at us. You will get a spanking when Papa Arturo finds out). His sister then replied, *"O sige! Dili na nako usbon and akong gi himo! Na nga yo bitaw ko ug kwarta sa atong Manong sa simbahan, dili man siya mang hatag bisag usa ka dako lang! Gi gutom na kaayo ko! Sige na gud! Kan un na nato ning saging!"* (Okay! I will not do it again! I did ask money from that Sir at the church but he did not want to give me anything even one cent only! I'm so hungry! Come on now! Let's eat these bananas!). Federico had no choice but to go along with his sister and ate the bananas that she shared with him.

One day, a miracle did happen during the sister and brother team daily trip to the church on the way home from school. As usual, even with all her pleading and frustration at our beloved Jesus Christ for not granting her wishes, my mother, Elizabeth still went straight to the statue to beg for money. But before she opened her mouth and flicked His feet, one cent fell off from Jesus' feet and landed into her tiny hands. Finally, Jesus Christ' crucified statue granted her wishes. This amazing occurrence through divine mercy scared little Elizabeth and made her cry, saying, *"Nong! Daghang salamat intawon sa imong regalo! Pa sai lua ko sa akong mga gihimo. Na a, na koy kwarta ron para ipalit namong mag suon ug pagkaon."* (Sir! Thank you very much for your gift! I'm sorry for what I have done. I have money now to buy food for me and my brother.) After she asked our Lord, Jesus Christ, for His forgiveness, after the miracle and blessing, He then surprised her by winking at her. At first, she wasn't sure whether she wanted to scream or run away. Instead of screaming from the top of her lungs, she decided to cry it out and then started running away from the church as fast as she could.

After another day passed by, she went back inside the church again, and this time she wanted to ask for more money. She wanted to test the statue to see if He would be kind enough to grant her more blessings which meant more coins. After positioning herself in her usual, daily routine, she said to the statue, *"Nong! Puede ba nimong dunga gan ang imong pag hatag sa kwarta? Himo ang duha ka centavos para daghan akong kwarta para maipalit nakog pagkaun. Ug mudaghan akong kwarta, maka ipon ko para may pang pliti namo ning akong ig suon para makita namo usab ang among inahan"* (Sir! Could you give me more money? Make it two cents more so I have money to buy food. And also, I will have enough money saved up to buy tickets for my brother and me to see our mother again). Miracles happen when you least expected it, lo' and behold, her wishes had been granted again. Not only had she gotten two cents this time, but she was granted five cents more as they fell off from Jesus Christ feet, and into her tiny hands. These miraculous incidents continuously happened every time she visited the statue of Jesus crucified. She was no longer afraid of the statue and she never ever flicked His feet again. In her innocent mind, she found a friend that would always be there and listen to her needs.

My uncle Federico and my mother were mistreated while living with their father, Mr. Ramsey and his extended family. Mrs. Ramsey made sure that everyday Federico and Elizabeth did almost all the household chores. As a reminder to Elizabeth and Federico of what Mrs. Ramsey whispered to them on the first day the two children moved in with them, they were not allowed to have school lunch allowances because according to their father, Mr. Ramsey, they had to work hard to earn their keep; he did not want his children to get used to having money in their pockets at a young age. But, of course, these house rules did not apply to his two children with Mrs. Ramsey because they were provided everything including school lunch allowances.

One school day, while in class, my mother's classmate went to the restroom and left her school bag at her desk. While her classmate was in the restroom, she stole the five *"centavos"* (cents) from her classmate's school bag and hid it under her tongue. The class subject was all about arithmetic. The teacher right away started the class by asking the students who can answer what was written plainly on the chalkboard. Most of the students were raising their hands except my mother. Consciously, the teacher then noticed that it looked like Elizabeth had something in her mouth. Out of curiosity, she asked Elizabeth to answer what was written on the chalkboard, *"Elizabeth! Unsa may sagot aning akong pangutana na one times one?"* (Elizabeth! What is the answer to my question, one times one?) Elizabeth can't answer the question because the coin that she stole was stuck under her tongue. In order for Elizabeth to escape from answering the question, she stood up, started crossing her legs, mumbled and shook her head, then pointed at her private part trying to tell her teacher that she needs to go to the restroom. When the teacher saw that she was serious, she then excused her and told her, *"O Sige! lakaw na!"* (Okay! Go now!) She ran so fast to the restroom and felt so relieved that she was able to escape from being caught stealing. Once she got into the restroom, she immediately swallowed the five cents coin and drank lots of water from the sink hoping she can excrete the coin later when she got home. By then, she did confidently believe that her classmates had already answered the math questions. But surprise-surprise, when she went back to the class, the question was still waiting for her. The teacher purposely reiterated the previous question, *"Elizabeth! Karon na naka ihi ka na! Unsa may sagot atong akong gipangutana na ko ganiha, one times one?"* (Elizabeth! Now that you have peed! What is the answer to the question that I asked previously, one times one?) She stood up with a conviction in her face and yelled the answer **"11!"** The class blasted out laughing because they knew that she was playing around to be funny. The teacher then realized that Elizabeth would not take her seriously, so she gave her another question, *"Elizabeth! Ayaw pag binuang kay ingnon nako ang imong amahan na nagpabuyag ka na pud! Tubaga ning lain nakong pangutana: two times two?"* (Elizabeth! Stop the foolishness because I will tell your father that you are misbehaving again!

Answer my other question: two times two?) Smart alec, Elizabeth then stood up again with a facetious look on her face and pause, *"Mam! Ang tubag a na ay 22!"* (Mam! The answer of that is **22!**) Again, Elizabeth's classmates laughed out loud. The frustrated teacher was so furious that as soon as Mr. Ramsey arrived to pick up Elizabeth, she told him immediately that Elizabeth was clowning again in her class. After she told him, my Grandpa Ramsey took his belt off and spanked Elizabeth's butt in front of her classmates and told her to apologize for misbehaving in her classroom. Once they got home, Grandpa Ramsey continued the punishment by asking his wife to sprinkle mongo beans in the living room corner floor to prepare for his daughter, Elizabeth to kneel on. My mother was still crying from the spanking she received, but when she saw the mongo beans on the floor, she literally cried out louder. She knew that this was another disciplinary way of her father by ordering her to kneel on the mongo beans with her arms extended in the air. Grandpa Ramsey was adamant in carrying out extreme punishment so that she would truly take her education seriously. Her daughter, Elizabeth kneeled continually for an hour until her knees started to bleed. That's when her father, Grandpa Ramsey asked her to stand up, go to her room to clean herself and then go to bed.

My mother had an unusual eating habit of sucking her food instead of chewing it. Every dinner time, when Mrs. Ramsey saw Elizabeth sucking her food, she automatically slapped her mouth hoping this would stop her silly habit. Sometimes, Mrs. Ramsey intentionally would not serve Elizabeth and Federico any kind of meat with their meal during dinner just to be mean to them. And once in a while, she would feed them under the dinner table like dogs.

One day, a woman was knocking on the door of my Grandpa Ramsey's house. He opened the door, looked at the woman's face and then noticed that she was holding the hand of a little boy while like a little secret agent, my mother was observing and watching behind the curtain hanging at her bedroom door. Grandpa Ramsey asked her, *"Kinsa man ka? Ngano man na may dala kang etum na bata sa akong balay?"* (Who are you? Why are you bringing a black kid into my house?) The woman responded, *"Mr. Ramsey, nung ning adto ka sa akong balay, nag iyotay man ta. Wa man ko maka hibaw na mamabdos diay ko."* (Mr. Ramsey, when you came by to my house, we had sex. I did not know that I would get pregnant.) But before the woman finished her story, Grandpa Ramsey put a halt in their conversation and asked her, *"Ha in man ka nakapuyo?"* (Where do you live?) The woman then had to mention the town's name. My Grandpa Ramsey mercilessly replied to her, *"Kadali lang usa! Kay katong imong gii-ngon na probensiya, wa pa man ko na kaadto did to. Dili man ko mo adto in ana ka layo. Laeng negro ang tatay anang imong anak. La kaw na, dayon!"* (Wait a minute! What you just mentioned about that province, I have never been there. I do not travel that far. I'm not the negro that fathered your kid. Leave, now!)

As a child, my mother had always been overactive in nature. When she was in first grade, she always picked a fight with the boys in her class. To her, it was fun playing marbles with them. One day, Elizabeth was playing marbles with one of the boys. When she started winning, he bullied her into taking her marbles from her hands and would not give them back to her. Feisty and daring little girl, Elizabeth was, she warned him, *"Ihatag nako'g balik nang akong giolin!"* (Give me back my marbles). But the boy did not believe her, so she grabbed, squeezed and pulled his penis until his face turned blue. When his mother saw what was happening through the window, she uncontrollably started screaming, *"Hunong *intawon! Nahimong asul ang naong sa akong anak! Maldita gyud kang bataa ka! Ako gyud kang isumbong sa imong amahan!"* (Please Stop! My son's face is turning blue! You are a very bad girl! I will tell your father!) That's when Elizabeth let go of his penis and started running fast back to her house. After the boy's mother comforted his son, they proceeded to walk down to my grandfather's house and told him the story of what transpired and that Elizabeth was the cause of her son's pain and suffering. Mr. Ramsey was stunned knowing what Elizabeth had done to her child. He was so furious that he promised her that this time, his daughter, Elizabeth will be severely punished. Grandpa Ramsey immediately called my scared mother, Elizabeth and spanked her in front of the boy and his mother and once again told her to apologize for what she did to him. Even though she apologized, she also told the mother that her son had been bullying her and stoled her marbles. But, her father, Mr. Ramsey did not believe her or even wanted to be entertained by listening to her story. After the mother and son left, Grandpa Ramsey quickly grabbed his daughter's hand and dragged her inside the house. He then asked his wife to get a rice sack. When his daughter, Elizabeth saw the rice sack, she furiously started screaming and crying loudly. While Grandpa Ramsey was holding her hands, he instructed Mrs. Ramsey to put holes in the sack and then open it so he can put her in. My poor mother was so helpless that all she could do is to keep crying and screaming, saying, *"Pa, intawon! Pasailua ko! Dili na nako himuun ug usab and akong gihimo. Ayaw lang intawon ko ug isulod sa sako! Maluoy ka Pa!"* (Pa, please! Forgive me! I will not do it again. Please do not put me in the sack! Have mercy Pa!) Grandpa Ramsey purposely ignored her pleas as he continued pushing her inside the sack and tied it up with the help of his wife. He punched more holes in the sack to make sure she had enough air for her to breathe. To make the punishment more extreme, Grandpa Ramsey took the rice sack outside the house and hung the rice sack on a tree which was infested with ants. My mother was helpless, unable to defend herself, continued to scream and cry while increasingly and loudly pleading, *"Pa intawon, Pa! Daghan kaayo ug lumigas! Gi katul na ko! Katul kaayo ang akong lawas, Pa! Intawon, Pa! Maluoy ka! Pasailua na intawon ko! Ma! Tabangi ko!"* (Pa, please, Pa! There are so many ants! I'm itching! My body is itching, Pa! Please, Pa! Have mercy! Forgive me, please! Ma! Help me!) She repeated her pleas over and over again but no one came to rescue her, not even her innocent brother Federico, because everyone was scared of Grandpa Ramsey. She cried and pleaded for hours until she no longer had the strength to cry. Her father and Mrs. Ramsey hung her from the tree for four hours until they did not hear her scream. All of sudden, all they could hear from the sac was my mother's softer sob and humming. When her father, Mr. Ramsey retrieved her from the tree, he then saw the fragile body of his little girl with severe ant bites all over her body. In the meantime, my uncle, Federico secretly ran to his mother, Liling's, house, and told her what their father and Mrs. Ramsey did to his sister, Elizabeth. My Grandma, Liling was so furious and outraged about the cruelty of what transpired. She dropped everything she was doing and told his son, Federico, *"Dinhi ka lang, dong! Kay mubalik ko dayon!"* (Stay right here, boy! I will be right back.) She went to the kitchen and grabbed a *"sundang"* (machete), wrapped her head in a colorful bandana (scarf) and started to stride towards the house of Mr. Ramsey. While she was walking in the street, the people got out of her way and no one dared to snatch the machete off her hand or stopped her to where she was going. My Grandma's eyes were bloodshot red with anger and ready to kill anyone who tried to stop her. Immediately, as soon as she arrived to Grandpa Ramsey's house, she began shouting, *"Gawas sa imong balay, ikaw, negro, anak sa gawas para patyon tika! Pesteng inatay ka! Karon na dayun! Ihatag nako ang akong anak kung gusto mong dili nako patyon kamong tanan dinha!"* (Step out of the house, you, black bastard so I can kill you! Damn mother fucker you! Right now! Give me my child if you don't want me to kill all of you!) Grandpa Ramsey stepped out of his house, scared and frantic while holding his daughter, Elizabeth's hand. He then pleaded Grandma, Liling to calm down. But before he handed her over to Grandma, Liling, he asked her to drop the machete on the ground. When my grandmother saw Elizabeth's frail and fragile look with a swollen face, she immediately dropped the machete and ran towards her. She instantly hugged her so tightly saying, *"Ginoo intawon! Kaluoy sa akong anak. Ginoo tabangi intawon siya! Sige lang day mupauli na ta."* (God have pity on my child! God, please help her! It's okay girl. We are going home.) Grandma, Liling then looked at his ex-man, Mr. Ramsey and angrily said, *"Dili ito ang atong katapusan! Pag bayaran ninyo ning gihimo nimo sa akong mga anak! Mga salbahi mo!"* (This is not the end! You will pay for what you have done to my children! You are mean spirited!) My Grandma, Liling, with one hand, picked up the machete and with the other hand, she held on tightly to Elizabeth's hand as they both cried uncontrollably on their way home.

As soon as they got home, Grandma, Liling asked her daughter, Elizabeth to take her clothes off so she could examine the severity of the ant bites. Surprisingly, Grandma, Liling was so shocked to uncover the swollen and spotted ant bites all over her body including her vagina. Grandma, Liling tried so hard to contain herself while sobbingly saying to Elizabeth, *"Sus Ginoo! Daghan kaayo ang imong paak sa lumigas pero nga no man ang imong bilat hubag pud kaayo?"* (My God! Your body has lots of stings from the ants but why is your vagina also swollen?) Her daughter, Elizabeth then responded, *"Si Papa ug ang iyang asawa gi sulod ko sa sakong bugas unya gibitay ko sa kahoy na daghang lumigas. Unya ang iyahang asawa, kahapon nag tadtad siya ug mga sili unya gibutang niya sa akong bilat para dili nako mu ki at"* (It's Papa and his wife who put me inside a rice sack and tied me up in the tree infested with ants. And yesterday, his wife minced all kinds of peppers and then slapped it in my vagina so I stop being naughty.) Grandma Liling was stunned and outraged! Filled with tears and her body trembling with anger and disbelief at how these people could be so cruel to her child. She applied an ointment to alleviate the swelling and to soothe the excruciating pain all over her body. Then Liling said, *"Sige day! Ihilak lang! kay wa man koy mahimo. Kailangan man nako tambalan tanan nako ang imong samad"* (It's okay girl! Cry it out! I have no choice. I have to apply this medication to heal all your wounds.) While Grandma Liling was slowly applying the medication, she kept sobbing and had to stop at times to catch her breath. This was as painful to her as much as it was painful to her loving daughter, Elizabeth. She wanted to go back out to kill both of them (Mr. and Mrs. Ramsey) but she had to think rationally about the future of the children without her. Why were Mr. and Mrs. Ramsey so cruel to her children when they are not able to defend themselves. Her daughter, Elizabeth was scarred and in excruciating pain for days because of the severe punishment she endured. She was not able to sit properly for days because of her swollen red vagina. For a little girl, these painful memories left a mark in her heart that haunted her for years.

From this time on, my mother, Elizabeth and my uncle, Federico went back to school under the supervision of my grandmother, Liling. On a regular school day, my mother, Elizabeth would deposit her books in her classroom and then went outside to sit under an acacia tree all day with her song hits book. In those days, the song hits book was a famous book filled with songs and lyrics with guitar chords. Every recess time, she went straight to the acacia tree and sat with her legs crossed reading the book religiously. There was no radio to listen to at that time. She had no idea what the tune of a song was and how she was supposed to sing it correctly. Although she was not privileged to enjoy listening to music at one point or another since her father, Mr. Ramsey did not allow her to listen to his radio, she was still amazingly able to create her own rhythm. When she lived with her father, sometimes she would sneak into the living room and turn on the radio before her father arrived from work. That was how she was then able to listen and learn what music and rhythm were all about. At the end of the school day, she picked up her books from her classroom and whistled happily all the way home, believing and feeling content with her day's accomplishments. The song hits music magazine was her school educational book. Even though Grandma Liling's children were now living with her, their father, Mr. Ramsey continuously checked the status of his children's education. Grandpa Ramsey knew that his daughter, Elizabeth was a very smart and strong headed little girl but his high hopes for her were to take education seriously and maybe become a prominent lawyer someday. But at the early age, my mother was naturally gifted in music and that's why she already instilled in her mind that someday, she would become a famous singer.

MYSTERIOUS ENCOUNTERS

On December 8, 1941, during the invasion of the Japanese, ten hours after the attack on Pearl Harbor in the United States, the Philippines were in the midst of fears and chaos. In 1942, during World War II, the Empire of Japan occupied the Commonwealth of the Philippines (based on the Philippine history). During the commotion in the Japanese War, my mother, Elizabeth and my uncle, Federico got separated from each other. When Grandma Liling picked up the kids from school, she only saw her shy son, Federico but could not find her clever daughter, Elizabeth. Without her knowledge, Grandpa Ramsey absconded his daughter, Elizabeth from her school and escaped into the forested mountain of Bagonbon (Bagonbon is located in Province of Negros Occidental, Western Visayas Region) to hide from the Japanese soldiers. Meanwhile, the Japanese military service members arrived in San Carlos City and started marching all over the city. In the middle of their search, they found out that the main source of the manufacturing industry of the city was sugar cane. The Japanese soldiers headed an investigation regarding the operation of San Carlos Sugar Milling Company. No one from the Japanese militants knew how to operate the equipment so they started questioning the locals on how to operate the sugar cane hand mill. The only way they could get a straight answer from the locals especially men was by intentionally torturing them. Hoping, eventually, someone would say something and provide them the name of the main operator of the hand mill. Because of the pain afflicted on one of the locals, he was left with no choice but to reveal the name of Mr. Arturo Ramsey. The militant then said, "That name does not sound Filipino, who is he?" He then revealed to the Japanese soldier that Mr. Ramsey was a United States Merchant Marine engineer who escaped from his shipyard and then settled in San Carlos City. The Japanese soldiers' commander then ordered a citywide search for grandfather, Mr. Ramsey. When my Grandpa Ramsey found out that there was a mass hunt search to bring him to the Japanese commander, he and his scared daughter, Elizabeth climbed up much higher than the forest mountains of Bagonbon to look for "Aetas" tribal group. Aetas are known to be the earliest inhabitants of the Philippine Islands. They are indigenous black people who lived in scattered, isolated mountains in the Philippine islands. These natives are called Negritos whose skin ranges from dark brown to black, of small stature and frame, hair of a curly to kinky texture. Knowing the native profiles, Grandpa Ramsey thought that his daughter, Elizabeth and he would be able to blend in with the tribes. The Aetas were literally so confused because my mother was not as dark as her father but willingly accepted them even though they knew that my Grandpa Ramsey's skin color was much darker than most of them. They were allowed to mingle with them for a while. The Japanese militants failed in their search for my grandfather, so they decided to use another way of locating him by dropping fliers from the fighter planes noting, "We need you to surrender Mr. Ramsey and report to the Central Milling Company." At this time, Grandpa Ramsey and his daughter, Elizabeth were more determined to stay with the Aetas. This was the only location they could be protected by the people who would not harm theirs.

One early dawn, my mother woke up at 5:00 in the morning, and her father, for some odd reason asked her to find wild tomatoes in the woods. She knew that she had to obey her father or there would be consequences. While she was searching for wild tomatoes in the forest, she fell asleep under a big tree. While asleep, she had a vision of a man wearing a white robe who called her name twice. She then said in her mind, "Oh! It's Jesus Christ!" She immediately followed the man in the white robe and felt like she was running but actually she was just walking behind him. Then all of a sudden, she woke up and found herself at the foot of the mountain. Then the man in the white robe from her dream disappeared. She realized it was already around noon time and she had not had any breakfast yet and there were no wild tomatoes to be found. As she continued walking, this time, she spotted a gigantic chicken. She followed this chicken, she threw stones at it to subdue it. After a while of chasing this animal, she noticed that she was outside the forest and that the gigantic chicken shortly disappeared. In reality, the chicken led her to where her mother, Liling, and her brother, Federico, were, which was a shelter by the river. Her eyes got so big and surprised at this miraculous nature of this phenomenon. She tried not to scream but just cried silently while approaching their shelter. They could not make a lot of noise because there might be Japanese soldiers around. My mother was finally reunited with her mother, Liling, and her brother, Federico, while her father, Mr. Ramsey still with the Aetas waiting for her return. Grandma Liling and her son, Federico were also glad to see her and thanked God for the blessing of this reunion. According to my mother, Jesus Christ had always been there for her, guarding and guiding her along the way.

In the year of 1945, the Philippine liberation celebrated after the United States aided the Philippine guerrillas to fight the Japanese soldiers. San Carlos City and other neighboring cities were now safe for everyone to go back home to start their normal household living. All academic institutions were now officially opened again for all students to go back to school. Liling, together with her children were so happy to be heading back to their own house. Mama, Elizabeth and Uncle, Federico was also excited to go back to school to see and play with their friends again. My mother still was not serious about getting an education. The only body of knowledge my mother wanted to invest in was in her singing and how to become a famous performer. She wholeheartedly believed that this was the only way for her to help her mother and brother to get out of poverty.

At the same time, my Grandpa Ramsey finally found his way back to San Carlos City and also reunited with his wife and their children. As soon as my grandfather settled back to his home, he instantly continued searching for his daughter, Elizabeth, because he had been longing for her forgiveness and attention. Consciously knowing that his daughter, Elizabeth was his most favorite little girl. One morning, while Grandpa Ramsey was searching for his daughter, Elizabeth, someone had told him that she was now enrolled in a public school. He then rushed to said public school to catch a glimpse of his loved daughter, Elizabeth and be able to talk to her after school. He wanted to offer her enrollment to a private school. First, my mother was so shocked to see her father and wondered what he was doing at her school. He slowly walked towards her and nicely presented his offer asking her if she would consider transferring to a private school and still be able to go home to her mother's house. My mother looked at him and bluntly said "No!" Not so much because she didn't want to go to a private school but because her mother, Liling, was again very sick of an unknown illness and that she needed to find ways to help buy her medications. She made a promise to herself that she would not give up finding the medicine that would cure her mother's illness. With God's grace, she would succeed in fulfilling her dream for her mother's sake.

ADULTHOOD

Elizabeth at the age of 16

In the year of 1947, my mother, Elizabeth growing maturely at the blossoming age of 16, finally, her ambition to be a singer came true. Her obsession with the song hits book paid off when she auditioned to be the lead singer of a local band and got hired. She spent long strenuous days learning the lyrics and melodies of the songs that the band wanted her to sing. She performed with the band from 9:00 in the evening until 6:00 in the morning at the local nightclubs. Because of her exhaustion, sometimes she found herself asleep on top of the drums. She needed 80 cents (centavos) to purchase the medicine for her mother which, fortunately, she was able to achieve. To broaden her experience, she continued to sing with other local bands and performed in various town plazas and fiestas.

In one of her gigs, her father, Mr. Ramsey saw her perform and once again begged her to not only go back to school to finish her education but also live with him. She finally agreed to his request to go back to school but with one condition; that she did not have to live with him. Meanwhile, Grandpa Ramsey was excited about her decision to go back to school, but at the same time, he was also disappointed that she was not going to live with his family. Immediately, he enrolled her again at St. Rita Catholic School; she only attended two weeks before dropping out, never to return.

This time, my mother went so far away from her father by boarding a ship going to Metro Manila, the capital region of the Philippines, with only two pesos in pocket money to survive. Determined and afraid, the little girl, my mother sought her dream to become famous in the big city of Manila. She sneaked into the ship pretending to be a waitress. At this point, she was ordered to bring a meal to the captain's quarter. The Captain right away noticed that she was scared. He then knew that she was not really a waitress but an illegal passenger of the ship. The Captain asked her, *"Kinsa man ka? Naka hi bao ko na wala kay plete. Naka hibao ka ba na puede ka ma biktima dinhi, unya lugoson ka, patyon ka, dayon pag hu man ihulog ang imong lawas sa dagat? Walang makahibao na nahitabo ni."* (Who are you? I know that you don't have a ticket. Do you know you can be a victim here, then you could be raped, killed, and have your body thrown out into the ocean? No one would ever know that this happened.) At this point, my mother got more scared than ever and started crying. She confessed to him and said, *"Sir, pasayloa ko intawon, ning dagan ko gikan sa San Carlos City para pakikipagsalaran sa Manila para ma palit nako ang nga tambal sa akong inahan ug matabangan nako siya sa among intaon kapobrehan."* (Sir, forgive me please, I ran from San Carlos City to adventure in Manila so I could buy the medicines for my mother and help her from destitution) While she continued sobbing, the Captain then felt sympathy towards her and wanted to calm her down. The Captain then said in a reassuring toned voice, *"Sige na dai, ayaw na ug sigig hilak. Na luoy ko nimo kay but an kang bata. Na ningkamot gyud ka bisag delikado ang imong kapalaran, maka tabang lang ka sa imong inahan. Sige! Kan a na lang ning akong pag-kaon kay gutom na kaayo imong naong. Pagkahuman, matuog kana dinha sa daplin. Pukawon na lang ka nako pag abot na to sa pantalan"* (Okay now girl, stop all that crying. I felt sorry for you because you are a good kid. You took a lot of risks even though your future is dangerous so you could help your mother. Okay! You can eat my food because your face looks so hungry. After this, go ahead and sleep in the corner. I will wake you up once we reach the pier). She then ate his meal and found a little corner to snuggle herself in with the blanket from the Captain's bed. After hours passed by, finally, the ship reached the shore, blew its horn preparing to dock at the pier. At this time, the noble Captain gently woke her up and ordered her to get ready to leave the ship. He generously gave her one peso as a token of his kindness and gave her the advice to take care of her money so she had money to feed herself when she got hungry. She was so appreciative of the Captain's gesture and thanked him profusely. She could not believe the goodness of the Captain towards her. Again, she thanked Jesus Christ for the blessings and for watching over her journey. Unfortunately, my mother never saw the Captain again throughout her lifetime.

Upon my mother's arrival in the city of Metro Manila, she quickly got a job as a live-in housekeeper. After a year as such, she was able to save some money and decided to pursue her dreams as a singer and later to join the band "Gintong Silangan." She was chosen as the lead singer of a six-man band. Since then, they were amateurs, who only contracted small gigs here and there. Every now and then, they would join a singing contest. The competition was so vicious and nasty that when they won, the competitors would throw rocks at them. Then they would run to the next town to sing and do other gigs like in Tondo and Malabon where the crowds were savage, brutal and treated them harshly. Whenever they made money, they split it among themselves which at the most was 10 pesos each. It was in Sampaloc where they joined a singing contest again and lost. Due to the failure to capture the solid appreciation of their audience on their performances, the band of six members sadly dismantled and went their separate ways. At this time, she ran out of money, so she decided to go back to her former employer as a housekeeper.

One day, there was a knock at the door and the owner of the house opened it. Surprisingly, the owner saw these two Black/Filipina women sisters named, Carol and Pat were asking for Elizabeth. The employer went to notify Elizabeth and told her that these women introduced themselves as her aunties. My mother was totally shocked and puzzled because she did not know that she had relatives living in Manila. She then ran downstairs, so excited to meet these ladies. But what a surprise! She was met with a slap in the face by one of the sisters and the other pulled her hair saying, *"Ano ka na Negra! Nakakahiya ka! Bakit pumasok ka ng katulong na trabaho? Hinahanap ka na nang mga magulang mo! Kaya kunin mo nang mga gamit mo para sumama kana sa amin!"* (What's up with you, black girl! You are embarrassing! Why did you get a housekeeping job? Your parents are looking for you! So, get your stuff now so you can come with us!) My mother was so stunned but she did not say anything and just went along with the drama. The employer encouraged my mother to go with them so the situation would not get out of hand and for Elizabeth not to be slapped again. She was taken aback by what just occurred, wondering what in the world was happening. My mother later found out that Carol and Pat were just rescuing her from her supposedly deplorable condition so that they could have her join with their Black/Filipina family circle. Another stunning development was when Elizabeth moved into Carol and Pat's house, she became their housemaid and did errands for them. She also met several other mixed black women like Channing, Viola, etc. These women lived in the segregated and poorest squatters' area in the Metro Manila. She thought Carol was a teacher because she always dressed up like a school teacher. Come to find out, these sisters were prostitutes and worked in the streets. But they treated her like their little sister. They loved and protected her from drugs, alcohol, gang members and cigarettes. They cared so much about her that they did not let her get out in the street without an escort from one of the sisters. The sisters knew that the street was not safe for an innocent young girl. The streets where they lived was infested with drug addicts, drug dealers, killers, and smugglers. My mother lived with them for several years, while trying to save enough money. Unfortunately, she did not get enough saved while living with them. Despite her living condition and financial struggle, she continued constantly learning the upcoming new songs. She practiced every day at her home hoping that one day the big break in show business would come true.

LIFE BEING MARRIED

Elizabeth at the age of 18

In her prime age of eighteen years old, my mother, Elizabeth, felt like her dream of being a singer did not flourish as she expected it to be. She was working hard but had no money to show for it. She then wrote a letter to her brother, Federico, to send her some money so she could buy a ticket for a boat fare to go back to her hometown of San Carlos City. She honestly told him that she was working as a housekeeper and still broke. Federico was now married with kids and was working at the Central Milling Company. Upon receipt of Elizabeth's letter, he was upset, appalled, worried and disappointed. He then immediately sent her 25 pesos. Once she received the money, she bought the ticket and broke the news to the sisters, Carol and Pat. She was so excited at the same time while telling the ladies that her brother, Federico, bought her a boat ticket to go back home because of their mother's health condition. Her mother, Liling, was severely sick and she also tremendously missed her. The sisters were sad that their adopted sister would be leaving them but at the same time happy that she would be reunited with her mother and be able to take care of her. They took her to the pier and that was the last time my mother saw her adopted truly loved sisters.

As soon as my mother arrived in San Carlos City, she was so thankful and excited to see her brother, Federico, and her mother, Liling, again. At this moment of time, Grandma Liling found the love of her life and decided to live with him and his name was Dominador Tabligan (aka Lolo Doming). My mother, Elizabeth, was so delighted and pleased that her mother finally fell in love and happy with a wonderful kind-hearted handsome man. Months passed by, and my mother, Elizabeth's, urge to sing and perform jump-started again. She started inquiring throughout San Carlos City and other neighboring cities who were looking for a band lead singer. Her determination paid off when several local bands recruited her to join them. They ended up traveling to different provinces, playing for plazas and fiestas. My mother was so adamant to make lots of money to help her mother out of poverty and be able to help pay for her constant supply of prescribed medications. At the same time, Lolo Doming, employment was working for a movie theater as the movie projector operator. In spite of his regular salary, he could only afford to supply the daily needs but not enough to support Grandma Liling's medications for her unknown illness. Grandma Liling's health condition began to worsen again and needed constant care and medication. She began losing weight and became very frail. In this unfortunate circumstance, my mother made the most desperate move of secretly meeting with her Father and asked for his financial assistance in order to buy her mother's expensive prescribed medications. Grandpa Ramsey was well known for having propositions before agreeing to anything. After she begged him, he proposed to her favorite daughter, Elizabeth, if she would agree to marry his good friend Isaac Johnson before granting her request. Grandpa Ramsey met Mr. Isaac Johnson way back when they were both stationed at Mactan, Island, serving under the United States Marine cargo ship. Out of the blue, their path crossed again and they rekindled their friendship when my grandfather visited Cebu. Surprisingly, Mr. Johnson was part of the demobilized team to stay in Cebu. Eventually, he ended his military service and decided to permanently stay in Cebu. Mr. Johnson was now looking for a good woman to spend the rest of his life with. In the middle of their rekindling conversation, Grandpa Ramsey happened to mention that he had a daughter who needed to settle down. What a coincidence that they saw each other again. Grandpa Ramsey then reiterated to his daughter, Elizabeth, that if she agreed to marry him (Isaac Johnson), then he would extend his assistance to help pay for her mother's prescribed medications. Her father told her, to let him know if she agreed to his proposition so that he could contact Mr. Johnson to make arrangements for him to come to San Carlos City.

Isaac Johnson, United States Merchant Marine

Desperate measures, and in a desperate situation that my mother was in. She was surprised and devastated that the only way for her father to help her was to give up her freedom of being single. She went back home and contemplated on her father's proposal. She told her brother, Federico about her secret meeting with their father and his father's wedding proposal for her to marry his friend Isaac Johnson. Uncle Federico was bewildered and speechless. He did not know what to say. She was asking for his advice on what to do. But days went by, and my mother still did not get any advice or guidance from her brother. All of a sudden, her brother, Federico, showed up and then said to her, *"Ikay bahala day, kay dili ra ba nimo kaila ning tawhana. Kung sa tanaw nimo na maayo siyang tao, para dili ka na mag kanta kanta bisag asa, pag-uyon na lang sa plano ni Papa. Unya simbako, ma nabdosan ka pa kay sige ka man ug biyahe."* (It's up to you girl because you don't know this person. If you think he's a good person, so you don't have to sing anywhere anymore, go ahead and agree to Papa's plan. God forbid, you may get pregnant because you are always traveling). What her brother was trying to tell her was to go ahead and get married so she could settle down. So that their mother, Liling, Lolo Doming and he would stop worrying about her whereabouts. She was always on the run looking for adventure. Grandpa Ramsey, as her father, was also worried about his daughter, Elizabeth's whereabouts and unstable destinations in life. One day, Grandpa Ramsey showed up at Grandma Liling's house to talk about his arranged wedding proposal to their daughter, Elizabeth, with his friend Isaac Johnson. Grandma Liling, just looked at him with a stunned face, so irate and couldn't believe what she was hearing from Grandpa Ramsey. She told him to get out of her house. She slammed the door and told him never to come back. Upon hearing the commotion, Elizabeth stepped out from her bedroom and told her mother that she agreed to his father's proposal. Grandma Liling's surprised reaction to what her daughter just agreed upon was absurd! Does she know that it was a stupid decision to marry a man she barely knew? Her daughter, Elizabeth, refused to reveal to her mother, Liling, the real reason behind her motive why she agreed to the arranged marriage. My mother did not want her mother to know that she just wanted someone to give her financial support so she could continually buy her prescripted medications. My mother proceeded to her father's house and told him her decision to marry Mr. Johnson. Without hesitation, Grandpa Ramsey called his friend, Mr. Johnson to come down to San Carlos City to meet his daughter, Elizabeth. A week later, Mr. Johnson traveled to San Carlos City to visit the house of Grandpa Ramsey. Tremendously anxious to meet the love of his life who was his friend's beautiful daughter who would be proudly handed to him for marriage. Grandpa Ramsey and Mr. Johnson walked to Grandma Liling's house ready to close the deal. My grandmother, Liling, opened the door which she knew what the visit for was, she called her daughter, Elizabeth, to come out from her bedroom to talk to her father. My mother was so scared and not excited because she would soon be married to a man that she barely knew. Grandpa Ramsey now proceeded to introduced Mr. Johnson to Grandma Liling. He then continued the introductory gesture to his son, Federico, and daughter, Elizabeth. Mr. Johnson kept staring at my mother while she had her head down. Mr. Johnson excitedly asked Grandma Liling's permission to marry her daughter. Grandma Liling, in turn, said, *"Basta and imong pag-taman kay Elizabeth, ug ang imong pagsaad nako na dili nimo siya sakitan."* (As long as you take care of Elizabeth and promised me that you will never hurt her.) Mr. Johnson then graciously promised to honor Grandma Liling's wishes. After the initial meeting, Grandpa Ramsey and Mr. Johnson left feeling satisfied with the outcome from Grandma Liling's house and headed back to my grandfather's house. My grandfather privately asked Mr. Johnson if he was truly ready to marry his daughter. Without reservation, Mr. Johnson said a big "Yes!" With excitement, Mr. Johnson formally then asked Grandpa Ramsey, for the hand of his daughter, Elizabeth, and promised to love her unconditionally. Grandpa Ramsey then said, "Okay!" and set the date for their wedding. Mr. Johnson then went back to Cebu City where he would wait for that special date.

"Here comes the Bride and Groom"

Marriage date: August 13, 1951
Elizabeth Ramsey: 19 Years Old
Isaac Johnson: 28 Years Old
Place of Marriage: San Carlos City, Negros Occidental

After the wedding ceremony, there was a small private reception. At the end of the gathering, my mother, Elizabeth with her new husband and soon to be my father, Mr. Johnson, headed to the hotel to consummate their marriage. My nervous mother felt so strange and had no interest whatsoever to submit herself to any sexual relationship with her husband. This situation was like a replayed episode of her mother's life experience. As soon as they got to their room, Mr. Johnson acted like a true gentleman by opening the door for her. He then proceeded to give my mother a big hug and kiss but she pushed him away. After her constant rejection, he continued to physically force himself on her. She did everything in her power to fight him off. She never thought that on the day of her wedding, her first physical encounter with her husband would result in her being raped. My fearful mother cried all night because she lost her virginity to a man that she barely knew instead of a man that she loved. She ended up sleeping on the floor, in pain and feeling ultimately violated. She did not want to sleep with a man that sexually assaulted her. She wanted nothing to do with her husband, so she kept one eye opened, guarding herself all night to be prepared for another unwanted sexual advance. Overwhelmed, by lack of sleep, she finally dozed off. After she woke up the next day, he was standing in front of her and told her that there would be no honeymoon. She innocently asked him, what is a honeymoon? He then said, do not worry about it. He then instructed her to get up and wash up so they could leave. The couple then headed to Cebu City where they were to begin their married life. Being a wife did not stop my mother from pursuing her dream and looking for a better life. She could not and would not give up her desire to be a singer.

A year later, my mother like her mother, Liling, was also scared and puzzled why her belly was getting bigger, why she was eating vigorously and always light headed. Mr. Johnson had to explain to her that she was pregnant. He had to elaborate his explanation to her, what pregnancy meant, and why she had a baby growing in her belly. Since they lived together as a married couple, Mr. Johnson was only financially providing her one-peso daily allowance which was not even enough money for her to save up for her mother's medication. Nine months later, she gave birth to a huge nine-pound baby boy named Isaac Johnson Jr.

Due to my mother's lukewarm attitude towards her husband and his forcible demands of her as a submissive wife, my father, Isaac, started having extramarital affairs which resulted in him fathering other children. Even though my father, Isaac, was unfaithful in their marriage, in his heart, he was still deeply in love with my mother. He continuously tried to create a more romantic relationship with her. She relentlessly rejected his advances because she had already made up her mind that she would eventually leave him to pursue her dream. Being married to him made her personal well-being so miserable and depressing. Shortly after their first child was born, my father was ready to make love with her but once again, she would physically refuse his intimate passion. One day after he returned home from work, unexpectedly, he carried her into their bedroom and once again forced himself on her. She was unsuccessful in defending herself. Some months passed by, after that last sexual encounter, she then discovered that she was pregnant again. This time, she gave birth to a beautiful curly eyed baby girl named, Mary Ann Johnson.

Years passed by, my mother was now taking care of two children. But my father was still financially supporting her with one peso a day. When their son, Isaac Jr., was six years old and daughter, Mary Ann, was five years old, she asked him to give her more money to take care of the household and their children or she would leave him and go back to her mother's house in San Carlos City. He then asked her, *"Pila man ang imong gipa ngayo?"* (How much are you asking for?) She replied, *"Tagai lang ko ug sitenta pesos! Kay dugay na nang mahurot ug naa koy ipalit na mga gamit para sa mga bata ug sa balay."* (Give me 70 pesos! Because that will last for a while and I want to buy things for the kids and for the house.) But in reality, she really wanted the money to purchase tickets for her and her kids so they could escape from him and go back to San Carlos City. My father, Isaac, being a clever man, played along with her and said, *"Sige! Ihatag nako ang sitenta pesos kong mo sugot kang mag iyotay ta!"* (Okay! I will give you the 70 pesos if you agree for us to have sex!) My mother thought of her plans and was so desperate to escape from her husband that she willingly agreed to his condition. For once, with no fighting to worry about, he was excited to express his love for her. After they had consented sexual pleasure, he then reached for his wallet and said, *"Tagaan ka nako lang ug trenta singko pesos. Sa susunod na nako ihatag ang tanang balancia kung musugot na pud kang mag iyotay ta."* (I will only give you 35 pesos. Next time, I will give you the remaining balance if you agree to make love again.) My mother felt so degraded and humiliated that all she could do was to cry and screamed, *"Inatay ka! Walay batasan ka! Demonyo ka! Dili gyud ka kamaayong tao!"* (Fuck you! Rude you! Devil you! You are a terrible person!) She then continued to cry excessively until he left and went back to work.

My father, Isaac, not being satisfied with his married relationship with my mother continued to cheat on her and had children with his concubine. One day, my mother just got back from the market when she overheard weird and moaning noises coming from the bedroom. When she opened the bedroom door, she was shocked and in disbelieve of what she saw. Her husband, Isaac, and their housemaid were having sex in their bedroom. My mother was so shocked that she froze and her body was trembling in anger. My father then turned his head around and looked at her and mumbled, *"Duol na kong mahuman! Guwa an nako!"* (I'm almost done! I'm climaxing!) She left the bedroom, ran towards the kitchen and grabbed a knife. She ran back into the bedroom wanting to kill both of them. Before she made it back to the bedroom, the housemaid had jumped out the window, naked as the day she was born, while her husband, Isaac, stood still, also naked and didn't know what to do. My mother then told him, *"Kung dili ka mulakaw ngayon dayon, patyon tika! Pesteng yawa ka! Wala gyud kay malecia! Alam kong nag babae ka! hantud dinhi sa balay nag iyot ka pa ug laeng babae? Unggoy ka! Ayaw nag isul ob nang imong sanina. Dad a na lang na!"* (If you don't leave right now, I'll kill you!

Damn devil you! You are very malicious! I know that you have other women! Even in our house, you fucked another woman? Monkey you! You don't have to put your clothes back on. Just take them with you!) My father, Isaac, was so ashamed and didn't know how to respond to her, he became suddenly motionless with fear. She was in the position to stab him even if he had made any sudden movement to defend herself. When she overheard the kids crying and screaming, she immediately diverted her attention to the kids. She dropped the knife and went towards the children. Isaac with a sigh of relief, thought that the kids will calm her down but he was wrong. She picked her son, Isaac Jr. by his neck and was about to drop him out the window. While the little boy's body was dangling out the window, she turned her head to her husband, Isaac, and screamed, *"Patyon nako ning bataa kung dili ka pa mulakaw karon dayon!"* (I will kill this child if you do not leave right now!) My father grabbed his clothes and ran from the house partially naked. You could hear the neighbors yelling and screaming outside the house telling my mother not to drop her child. As soon as her husband left, one of the neighbors came upstairs and went inside the house to comfort her and to negotiate with her. The heroic neighbor then said, *"Ayaw intawon day! Wala may kalibutan ang mga bata sa nahitabo karon! Ning lakaw na bitaw ang imong asawa. E butang na intawon ang imong anak. Sige na dai! Kaluoy intawon sa imong anak!"* (Please girl, don't do it! The child had nothing to do with what happened today! Your husband already left! Put your child down please! Please girl! Please have mercy on your child!) She was so distraught that she attempted to kill her only son, Isaac Jr., while her vulnerable little daughter, Mary Ann, who witnessed the entire drama in front of her innocent eyes, kept crying. Finally, my mother calmed down and put her son on the floor and gave him a big hug. Meanwhile, Mary Ann ran towards her mother and she also gave her a big hug. My heartbroken mother then said, *"Pasay loa ko mga anak.*

Pasayloa ko intawon. Mahal na mahal ko intawon kamo." (Forgive me my children. Forgive me please. I love you very much.) My mother and my brother and sister shed tears all day to express their pain and suffering. The heroic neighbor began to speak out saying, *"Sige hipusa na inyong mga gamit karun dayon para maka lakaw namo bag-o maka balik ang imong asawa."* (Okay pack up your things now so you can leave before your husband gets back.) My mother, Elizabeth, and her children, Isaac Jr., and Mary Ann quickly packed enough belongings that they could take with them. They rode on a pedicab (a small pedal-operated passenger bicycle, like a taxi service) heading towards the pier.

ADVENTURES

At this point, my mother, Elizabeth, temporarily separated from her husband. She and her children, Isaac Jr. and Mary Ann, finally arrived in San Carlos City to live for a while with her mother, Liling, and step-father, Doming. Few months passed by, my mother got the urge again to pursue her career in singing and to be a famous singer in the big city of Metro Manila. One morning, she asked her mother, Liling, if she could talk to her about her plans to go back to Manila. After all her daughter had been through, Grandma Liling was surprised that she would still want to pursue her singing career in Manila. My mother was trying to justify that singing was the only job she knew how to support her children financially. Even though my Grandma Liling disapproved of her reasoning, she had no choice but to let her go to fulfill her dream. No matter how much her mother, Liling, convinced her to stay, she would still pursue her desire to leave San Carlos City. To give her the reassurance, Grandma Liling told her not to worry about the children because she and Lolo Doming would take care of them. The following week, my mother was anxious to leave town to make her dream come true.

The only affordable vessel for day to day short-trip transportation my mother could take traveling to Manila was a passenger carrier. While she was on the ship, she started feeling sick and vomited constantly. She thought that it might just be a sea sickness but when she looked at her belly, it seemed like it had been gradually growing. That was when she realized that she was pregnant again with her third child, who happened to be yours truly! She was so mad, disappointed and worried about how she could start her singing engagements if she was pregnant again. She decided to seek a housekeeping job for a while until she gave birth or maybe found a way to abort the child. She was then hired by a lady named Lourdes. Lourdes' was a midwife (the main caregiver to childbearing women) who also gave medical assistance to those having difficulties with their pregnancy. Lourdes' regular patients were prostitutes who wanted their unborn child aborted so they could go back on the street right away. Although some of them wanted to keep their babies to stop prostituting. My mother obviously did not reveal the information right away to Lourdes about her pregnancy. Lourdes instructed her that the job was not just housekeeping but also giving medical assistance to her midwifery business. Again, God worked in mysterious ways because of all the traditional households, she ended up working for a midwife and a household that takes care of pregnant women. But my mother obviously had something else in mind, she tried to have a miscarriage by scrubbing the floors every day with a coconut husk called "bunot" (Visayan word for a traditional Filipino cleaning and polishing tool to scrub wooden floors). Scrubbing wooden floors with "bunot" every day is a very strenuous regiment that can cause one to lose weight or in my mother's case, it could threaten the life of the fetus which would result in a miscarriage. Months passed by, and her belly kept growing and now started to show more from her dress. Out of curiosity, Lourdes asked her, *"Day! Buntis ka ba?"* (Girl! Are you pregnant?) She looked at Lourdes with her terrified expression, and then she had no choice but to confess, *"Opo! Hindi ko po alam kung paano ko sabihin sa inyo. Ayaw ko pong sanang matuloy itong pag bubuntis ko kasi ayaw ko na pong magka anak sa asawa kong walang hiya. Uminom na ako nang mga pang lason na mainom galing sa inyong medisinang kabinete, lumalaki pa rin siya. Nag lampaso na po ako araw-araw wala pa rin pong nang yari. Ayaw ko na po talagang manganak. Hindi ko na po alam kung ano na ang dapat kong gawin. Tulungan ninyo po ako."* (Yes! I did not know how to tell you. I did not want to continue my pregnancy from a cad husband. I drank lots of poisonous drinks from your medicine cabinet, still, the baby is growing. I scrubbed the floors everyday still nothing happened. I really don't want to give birth. I don't know what to do anymore. Please help me.) Luckily, and perhaps God's will, she did not succeed in losing the unborn child. The unborn child clung tightly to her womb. She begged Lourdes to help her abort the child. She honestly told her that she could no longer afford to raise another child and especially because of all the things she had been through in her marriage. Feeling sorry for her, Lourdes finally gave in and scheduled the abortion procedure. On the day of the procedure, as Lourdes was about to insert the uterine curette into Elizabeth's vagina, a mysterious lightning struck from nowhere in between Elizabeth's legs. As fear engulfed Lourdes, she suddenly stopped the procedure, and while frightened, she said in a frantic voice, *"Day! Ang kidlat ay senyas galing sa Diyos! Gustong mabuhay nitong batang ito! Pasensiya ka na! Hindi ko pueding ituloy! Sige mag bihis kana kasi gawa nang Diyos na ayaw niyang matanggal ko ang batang ito."* (Girl! The lightning is a sign from God! This child wants to live! I'm sorry! I cannot proceed! Go ahead put your clothes back on because it is God's will that he did not want me to abort this child.) My mother felt so puzzled with the acceptance under the control of God's grace, started crying and said**,** *"Opo! Ituloy ko na lang po ang pagbuntis ko. Wala po akong magawa kung ito ang gusto nang Diyos."* (Yes! I will continue my pregnancy. There's nothing I can do if it's God's will.) Lourdes in turn, gladly offered her services by promising to help her deliver the child with no cost. Since that miraculous intervention, my loving mother started to pray to Jesus of Nazareth, wishing to grant her a miracle regarding her singing career.

One hot day, she was listening to the radio and suddenly she heard that there was a singing contest in a radio program called "CBN Canteen" (A 1958 radio show on DZXL, hosted by Eddie Ilarde, Bobby Ledesma, Bobby De Vera and Leila Benitez. The name of the show was changed into "Student Canteen" because it became a nationwide hit with students). Even though she was already seven months pregnant, she wanted to take a chance and secretly entered the contest. She asked Lourdes if she could enter in a radio show singing contest. Lourdes without hesitation approved and supported her request. She then went to the radio station and signed up. She decided to wear a dress that would not show her big tummy. Unfortunately, she lost and she went home so hurt and disappointed. As soon as she got home, she told Lourdes the bad news and went straight to her bedroom and prayed again to Jesus of Nazareth, *"Ngano man ang ubang tao mo daog man bisag dili sila makahibayong mukanta? Bakit ba dahil maganda sila kahit sintunado silang kumanta? Ngano man dili gyud ko maka daog? Dahil ba na pangit at negra ako? Sige na Senor Nazareno; tulungan mo akong manalo kasi ma itim ka rin!"* (Why is it that other people are winning even though they can't sing? Is it because they're pretty even though they cannot sing in tune? Why is it I couldn't win? Is it because I'm ugly and black? Come on Señor Nazareth; please help me win because you are also black!) Her way of praying was so powerful and it was from the heart with an attitude. She cried and cried while praying and kept asking, *"Bakit? Bakit? Ngano man? Dahil ba na petong buwang buntis ako? Dahil ba na wala akong magandang damit na ma e suot?"* (Why? Why? Is it because I'm seven months pregnant? Is it because I don't have a nice dress to wear?) She kept crying all night until she fell asleep. Days passed by, then all of a sudden, she heard a band next door practicing. She was so amazed but puzzled because they did not know how to play the arrangement of the songs. Their singing and music playing sounded off key. She then knocked on their door and introduced herself. She was so excited to meet them that she volunteered to help them arrange the songs that they were rehearsing. The band leader asked her if she was interested to join the band and be their lead singer. Without reservation, she gladly accepted the offer in spite of being pregnant. She kept rehearsing with the band until nine months into her pregnancy.

On December 28th, Lourdes delivered the baby girl named Susan (yours truly!). According to Wikipedia: In the old days, December 28th is celebrated as "Innocence Day" which commemorated the massacre of the children by King Herod in his attempt to kill the infant Jesus, (Matthew 2:16-18). These children were regarded by the early church as the first martyrs. But it was uncertain when the day was first kept as a Saint's Day. At first, it may have been celebrated with Epiphany. But by the 5th century, it was kept as a separate festival. In Rome, it was a day of fasting and mourning. When a child is born on this day, they also could be named Innocencia for girls and Inocencio for boys. Lourdes then graciously asked my mother if she was going to name her child Inocencia since she was born on Innocence's Day. With one quick glance at me, my mother said, "Hell no! I will name her Susan." When I was born, I was "in the caul" or birth in an unruptured amniotic sac. According to Wikipedia – "A child born with a caul is rare. Occurring of this kind of childbirth is fewer than 1 in 80,000 births. In medieval times, the rare appearance of a caul on a newborn baby was seen as a sign of good luck. It was considered an omen that the child was destined for greatness. Gathering the caul onto paper was considered an important tradition of childbirth; the midwife would rub a sheet of paper across the baby's head and face, pressing the material of the caul onto the paper. The caul would then be presented to the mother to be kept as an heirloom. Folklore in tells developed suggesting that possession of a baby's caul would give its bearer good luck and protect that person from death by drowning. Cauls were, therefore, highly prized by sailors, and medieval women often sold these cauls to sailors for large sums of money; a caul was regarded as a valuable talisman." This tradition was also customarily practiced in the Philippines during my birth year. Unfortunately, Lourdes knew about this practice and she took advantage of the situation. While my mother was delivering me, she carefully removed the translucent inner lining tissue tightly wrapped around my body and stole it. She knew the benefit of having it as a good luck charm, but she neglected to understand that the good luck charm only works if it's given to the mother of the child, or it will turn into a curse. My mother knew what Lourdes did but she couldn't say a word about it because she was my mother's employer. Regretfully, after Lourdes stole the caul, her life went into a downward spiral and she suffered from incurable illness.

DREAMS DO COME TRUE

Three days after I was born, my mother, Elizabeth, convinced the band to audition for a radio show called "Student Canteen." They named the band "Star Glow" which consisted of four men and her as the lead singer. After the band auditioned, they immediately qualified to be one of the contestants. They were so amazing that they became four times undefeated champions of Student Canteen talent show. The audience members consisted predominantly of students from different universities. The audience always wanted an encore every time they performed by screaming and loudly chanting their name – "Star Glow! Star Glow!" They were so well received by the audience, to the point that their single song performance turned into a full-length concert in an amateur talent show. They ended up singing seven songs by that time, the emcees had to put an intermission in the program. The scheduled emcees were Eddie Ilarde and Leila Benitez. Leila whispered encouraging words to Elizabeth, saying, *"Sige lang day! Bumalik ka nang bumalik sa entablado at kanta lang kayo. Baka dumating ang panahon sumikat ka."* (Go ahead, girl! Keep going back to the stage and you keep singing. Maybe the day will come that you will be a star.) Since the audience did not stop yelling for more Star Glow, other guest performers like Ike Lozada (became a famous comedian, actor and TV host) and Pepe Pimentel (became famous game show host and actor) were not able to perform at all until the amateur show was over. Another musical composer, Phil Delfino, was curiously eyeing Elizabeth's talent and her remarkable performance. He murmured to her after the show, *"Beth! Balang araw, sisikat ka talaga!"* (Beth! Someday, you will be a star!) To respond to his kind wishes, she told him, *"Tito Phil, malayo ko pong tangkaing ang mangarap na sisikat ako."* (Uncle Phil, it's too far for me to reach my dream to be a star.) My mother always proudly acknowledged that her talent was miraculously granted to her by the Jesus of Nazareth.

Days shortly after the successful run of gigs with the band, finally, my mother had the courage to move out from Lourdes house to look for her own residence. She found a small studio style apartment to move into by renting it for 15 pesos a month. She continued to sing with the Star Glow band until she met a lady named Viola who became her friend and also her primary babysitter. Like my mother, her friend Viola was also married to a United States military serviceman. My mother would also sometimes ask some of the ladies in the neighborhood when Viola was not available to babysit me. They became such close friends of my mother that eventually, she asked these ladies to be my Godmothers in my baptismal ceremony. But my mother still felt that something was definitely missing. She was also looking for someone to be my Godfather. The first person that came to her mind was a well-known wealthy man who always hung around Harrison Street. She approached him and bluntly asked him, *"Gusto po ninyo maging Ninong nang anak kong babae?"* (Would you like to be the Godfather of my daughter?) His first reaction was that a surprise; that he, a total stranger was asked to assume all legal stewardship of a child should something happen to the biological mother. After my mother's several attempts at persuading him to do it, he eventually agreed to be the Godfather. Now that my baptismal Godparents had been selected and agreed upon, my baptismal ceremonial then took place. Unfortunately, months after the baptismal ceremony, the wealthy man, according to rumors, later became an alcoholic, and was never seen again.

SUCCESS

After I was baptized, my mother, Elizabeth, asked my Grandma, Liling, to move in with us to help take care of me. It was at this time that she needed a full-time babysitter for me so she could travel to sing without worrying. Grandma Liling had to get permission from her live-in man, Lolo Doming because he would end up to be the only babysitter of their other grandchildren, Isaac Jr. and Mary Ann. After my mother's plea, to Grandma Liling, she had no choice but to help her beloved daughter to take on another grandchild. In a lighter note, Grandma Liling was also excited to raise a granddaughter whom she had never seen. Weeks later, after the assured commitment from Lolo Doming to take care of their other grandchildren, Grandma Liling then left to travel also through a carrier from San Carlos City to the city of Manila to live with us in a very small studio apartment. The living accommodation was so limited that the area was one room which also included the bathroom. She continued to travel performing with the Star Glow band and was able to earn enough money to pay the rent and other household expenses. While performing with the band, my mother decided to audition again as a soloist at the next Student Canteen competition where she won multiple times and became the undisputed champion. As a Student Canteen guest winner, she was rewarded with sets of giveaway gifts: small cups, plates, utensils, drinking glasses and a box of evaporated milk. Every time she fed me the evaporated milk, I immediately started vomiting and had constant diarrhea. My mother always ended up taking me to the doctor. On her fourth winning streak, my mother refused to accept any more of the evaporated milk, and boldly told the Student Canteen production staff that it made her daughter sick. When the radio listeners heard her comment, it affected the show sponsorship rating. The comment did horrendous damage that upset all the Student Canteen promoters and sponsors and was the biggest reason for my mother to be dropped from the show. But what a coincidence because before she was purged from Student Canteen, someone by the name of Renee, (the brother of Chiquito, a famous legendary Filipino actor and comedian) came by at the radio station that day and advised my mother to audition at the Opera House. She innocently told him, *"Opera House ay para lang sa mga operatic na manga nganta!"* (Opera House is only for an operatic singer!) Renee laughed out loud and said, *"Beth, dalhin kita duon, para makita mo ano talaga ito."* (Beth, I will take you there, so you will see what it's all about.) She agreed to his offer and went home feeling accomplished with everything that took place that day. What happened to my mother was a very good example of a very famous quote: "When one door closes, another one opens!"

The first dress that my mother wore at the Opera House audition was given to her by a generous seamstress from the neighborhood whose husband was an engineer from Guam. They were a middle-class family who owned their own home, as well as a grocery store and on the side as a hobby, she liked to sew dresses. She told my mother that if she ever ended up on a big stage show, she would sew her first dress, and she did keep her promise. My mother still remembers the dress that was made for her; it was a white dress with ruffles around it. Through all these years that passed by, she felt bad that she never had the opportunity to go back to the seamstress' house and thank her again. She was not sure if she was still alive because she could not find her and did not remember her name. It was a struggle for my mother to go back to Lourdes' house because it reminded her of the painful memories, at the time when she had to make one of the most difficult decisions in her life – to either keep the child or not. My mother's motto was that you cannot linger in the past if you want to go forward in life. Her long struggles and painstaking effort to excel in her talent became a reality when she passed the audition at the Opera House and was hired by Mr. Lou Salvador Sr. He was then the master showman at the Opera House. My mother's lifelong dream came true when she became a regular Opera House stage show performer rendering songs of multiple American rock n' roll legends like Little Richard, Buddy Holly, Chuck Berry, Bill Haley and the Comets, Chubby Checker and Elvis Presley.

In the year of the 1950's through the 1960's, there were only been two rivalries of live stage shows theaters in major Manila area: Manila Grand Opera House, which located at Recto Avenue, and the Clover Theater at the foot of Jones Bridge. The two theaters were in alongside Rizal Avenue and featured the top of the best local singers, dancers, and actors, which included the foreign entertainers.

In the year of 1959, my mother asked Lolo Doming to move to Manila with my brother, Isaac Jr. and my sister, Mary Ann. We all moved into a very rugged house with walls and floors made out of bamboo full of holes. After my mother had saved enough money, she asked us to get ready to move out again. But this time into a little decent apartment in Santol which we rented for 150 pesos a month. One day, one of my mother's friends asked her if she would be interested to move into his previous apartment. Without hesitation, my mother took the offer because it was the best deal. She would be moving into an apartment which was bigger than the previous one, a better neighborhood and on top of it, she would be paying the same rent of 150 pesos a month. After all, our moving situation became normal for whatever makes sense or affordable to my mother, we have no choice but to follow her lead.

My mother continued her performances at the Manila Grand Opera House for many years. She became so popular from her stage show performances, that the news reached to the rival Clover Theater. When Mr. Don Jose Sarah, the Portuguese producer and stage director of the Clover Theater, bought a ticket at the Opera House Theater to watch my mother perform, he was fascinated. He waited for her to finish her gig, and he was so excited to finally meet her. He then offered her a proposition that if she decided to move to the Clover Theater, he would pay her to double the salary of what she was earning at the Opera House. My mother was so ecstatic and just looked at him like she had seen an angel. With no reservation, she accepted the offer right on the spot. On the same night, she said goodbye to Mr. Lou Salvador Sr. It was a very interesting, true story of how consequently she was named, The Philippine Queen of Rock N' Roll. Well, let me tell you: Mama was so stressed from us constantly moving around from place to place that it badly affected her voice. Not just the moving around but worrying about our living conditions, the well-being of her children, Grandma Liling and Lolo Doming. On top of that, her strenuous work schedules, singing sixteen songs per show, and three shows a day. It started to affect her singing voice, as it sounded rugged and gruff, not like a typical little lady's voice. Her voice and sound became a hit with the audiences. Therefore, Clover Theater labeled her as the Philippine's Queen of Rock N' Roll.

One day, she received the bad news that her husband, Isaac Johnson Sr. had died on April 11, 1959. After she left Mr. Johnson, he became alcoholic and suffered from heart complications which eventually became the cause of his death. But before his passing, he petitioned all his three children (Isaac Jr., Mary Ann & me) to become American citizens. After his memorial, my mother received a letter from the United States addressed and processed by the Philippine Embassy as the liaison between the United States government and the Philippine government. My mother had to appear at the Philippine Embassy to sign the documents and comply with all the requirements needed to complete the process of her children to receive full benefits as citizens of the United States. We became American citizens having one of the benefits that we could still be able to continue to live in the Philippines. The condition was that we had to leave the Philippines before our 21st birthday to exercise our American citizenship. The only exemption granted was if we were finishing our college education; once we graduated we could leave. My mother was so happy and felt fortunate that at least her children would have a chance for a better future. Looking back at all the dreadful, horrific things that my father had done to her, they were overshadowed by the loneliness and sadness she felt after my father's death that she was finally able to forgive him. In the end, my mother wanted to thank him by saying, "Let bygones be bygones, Isaac! May God bless your soul and may you rest in peace."

In order for my mother to save up money and be able to support her family, her regular way of transportation was a jeepney (popular Philippines cultural public transportation) instead of a taxi cab when she went to perform at the Clover Theater. Her work regular daily regiments were: eating only once a day with "tuyo" (stinky dried fish) with rice and multiple cups of coffee. Sometimes she indulged herself by eating fresh eggs for stamina to sustain her strength, to be able to perform three shows a day, and be able to sing sixteen songs per show. Her famous saying was, *"If God wants you to survive, it does not matter how often you eat in a day, you will survive."* She became Mr. Sarah's favorite performer and employee. Most of the other performers would always ask for advance payments every week except her. Many of the performers owed Mr. Sarah money because most of them were not able to catch up with the payment plan. They always borrowed money from Mr. Sarah two days after their performances. By the time they got paid and made payments on their bills, they had no more money again to repay Mr. Sarah. In turn, they ended up asking for another advance payment to survive for the week. My mother was not an angel herself either. She had a habit of not showing up to perform when if she did not feel like it. This diva attitude happened only twice. One day, Mr. Sarah called her into his office to have a private meeting. He took off his belt and spanked her butt liked she was a little kid. She was so shocked and asked him why? Mr. Sarah replied, "You are a very stubborn woman, you have three children to support, and if you do not listen to me and be absent again from your scheduled performances, you will not be allowed to perform in my theater again." After that incident, she never missed any performances again. Mr. Sarah then learned to love and appreciate her commitment which improved their working relationship. After years of managing the Clover Theater, Mr. Sarah finally decided to go back to Portugal. Everyone was so sad, especially his right-hand man, and good friend, Mr. German Moreno (he became a TV talk show host & movie actor). Before Mr. Sarah departed, my mother gave him an assurance that "When you leave, I will not work for any theater again. I will find my way to seek other opportunities, like what you told me. I will teach myself to make sacrifices in order to succeed."

In the year of 1961, the "Philippine Festival", a huge, spectacular musical show produced by Mr. Steve Parker, the husband of Ms. Shirley Maclaine (the famous Hollywood star), was performed at the Dunes Hotel, Arabian Room at the city of Las Vegas in the United States. My mother was hired to perform along with the following performers: Pilita Corrales, Shirley Gorospe, Jun Aristorenas, Ramon Zamora, Bobby Gonzales, Baby Aguilar, Boy Pecson, Betty George, etc. My mother was one of the highlights of the show and on the same level with the other stars like Al Quinn, Alice Reyes, Ricardo Reyes, conductors, and 75 island maidens. The extravagant show was directed and choreographed by Mr. Paul Godkin. My mother was not even aware that she was hired to be the star of the musical show. Until one day, there was a big commotion with the group, when it was revealed that my mother was the star. She was so busy playing games at the slot machines that it had never dawned on her to ask why she was always performing at the end of the show. On one special occasion, Harry Belafonte found out that there was a Jamaican singer performing at the Dunes Hotel. He decided to cancel one of his shows to watch the fabulous

Philippine Festival show to witness the performance of this amazing Jamaican woman. After the show, Mr. Harry Belafonte went backstage and congratulated my mother. He picked her up and gave her a big hug. He was so mesmerized by her performance and was so proud of her Jamaican descendant. On different occasions, my mother was also congratulated by Mr. Sammy Davis Jr. and Mr. Elvis Presley backstage after the show. That's when all the jealousy of the group came about. She became the favorite of Mr. Steve Parker. She recalled that their group experienced the civil rights injustice in the United States in the 1960's when minorities were not allowed to enter at the front entrances of the hotel but to enter from the back of the hotel. One day, the group decided to venture outside the Dunes Hotel and wanted to dine at a neighboring restaurant. When they went inside the restaurant and sat down to be served, the waitress refused to serve them because of their race. For them, such a rude attitude only confirmed the existing struggle of minorities in the U.S. They had no choice but to go back to the hotel, entering through the back door.

When she got back from Las Vegas, Grandma Liling, Lolo Doming, my brother, my sister and I, decided to leave Manila to move back to San Carlos City, Negros Occidental to live permanently. Manila was just too hectic and too big for a city to live in. Grandma Liling and Lolo Doming were used to simple living. Since my mother not by her choice, had to live alone, she decided to move in with Mr. Manning Lagunsan, a newspaper tabloid owner. She stayed with him and his family for awhile until she decided to go back to San Carlos City and to live with her us again. My mother brought lots of gifts including the pension benefits documents for us from the Philippine's U.S. Embassy. She stayed in San Carlos City for a while and converted the corner of our house into a little modest sari-sari store (a neighborhood convenient store) operated as a small business for extra income to supplement our daily living. Again, my mother realized that she needed to go back to Manila in order to support her family. Her means of livelihood in Manila was in showbiz. She just could not contain herself not to be in show business. It was another sad moment because she had to say goodbye again to her mother, step-father, and us, her children. That was one of the hardest farewells she had to do.

Sari-Sari Store with Liling in the background – Susan, Mary Ann and cousins, and friends were the children

Sari-Sari Store with Liling, Susan and family members

FAITH

In the year of 1962, at the age of 31, my mother, Elizabeth, was asked to campaign for then-Senator Ferdinand Marcos, before he became the President of the Philippines. She was hesitant to get involved in politics, but she knew that there might be something beneficial, so she decided to get involved with Mr. Marcos' campaign. The day came for Mr. Marcos to return the favor. She made a private appointment to speak with him to have a one-on-one meeting in his office. What she was about to ask him would be the hardest and most unthinkable requested by a daughter regarding her father's citizenship status because of her deepest animosity towards Grandpa Ramsey. She bluntly requested to extradite her father to the U.S. government because he unlawfully vacated from his military ship, and needed to be deported back to the United States Marine base. The legal document for deportation had to be personally signed by Mr. Marcos and be sent or she could personally deliver the document to San Carlos City Municipal Court which would have jurisdiction over the case. Mr. Marcos was puzzled, on why she wanted to deport her own father. My mother then explained the family history and her bitterness towards her father which caused considerable pain and suffering she had endured from him. She explained to the senator that this was a personal "vendetta" (revenge) for all the punishment and hardship that her father had done to her mother. Mr. Marcos felt that she was sincere with her emotion and truly wanted to give closure to her unfortunate memories. She paused and started crying because it brought back painful memories. She made a firm decision to seek closure to a family matter. Mr. Marcos just had a shocked look on his face. He stared at her for a minute and asked her, *"Ms. Ramsey, ito ba talaga ang gusto mo?"* (Ms. Ramsey, are you sure this is really what you want?) He suggested that maybe she should have first a small family meeting with her mother, stepfather, and her kids before pursuing the deportation process. But all she could say was, *"Tiyak ako tungkol sa desisyon na ginawa ko at walang sinuman ang maaaring magbago ng aking isip."* (I'm certain regarding the decision I have made and no one can change my mind.) He then told her to stay in his office because he needed to consult with his legal team if the legal document that he was about to approve and sign would be legally binding to a specific deportation process for an American soldier. Thirty minutes passed by, still no sight of Mr. Marcos. While my mother was anxiously waiting, the quietness of the office surroundings did not help her state of mind because it made her nervous to the point where she started to second guess her decision. As the office door opened, she saw Mr. Marcos walking towards her. All of a sudden, she went back to her assertive authoritative attitude and look. In her mind, upon receipt of the legal document, there was no turning back. Mr. Marcos hesitated in handing her the document and asked her one last time if she was absolutely sure she wanted to proceed with this matter. She replied, *"Oo Sir, kailangan kong gawin ito upang makapagpatuloy ako sa aking buhay."* (Yes Sir, I have to do this so I could move on with my life). Before Mr. Marcos handed her the legally approved and signed document, he said, *"Ms Ramsey, I'm sorry tungkol sa kung ano ang nangyari sa iyo at sa iyong pamilya. Umaasa ako na ang tulong na ito ay magdadala sa iyo ng ilang pagsasara tungkol sa iyong bagay na pampamilya upang mabawasan ang iyong sakit at pagdurusa lalo na ang iyong mapagmahal na ina."* (Ms. Ramsey, I'm sorry about what happened to you and your family. I hope this helps bring you some closure regarding your family matter to ease your pain and suffering especially your loving mother). She then gave him a big hug, and as a parting word, she said, *"Maraming salamat, Sir! At ngayon ay ipaglilingkod ang hustisya!"* (Thank you so much, Sir! And now justice will be served!)

Days passed by, after that private meeting with Mr. Marcos, my mother was now ready to bring justice to the oppressors. She started preparing her travel back to San Carlos City to finally put to rest everything that she had felt about Grandpa Ramsey and Mrs. Ramsey. A week before her departure date, even though she still had vindictive feelings towards her father, she still wanted to give him something from the fruits of her labor. She bought him a T-shirt and slippers from one of the places she had traveled as *"pasalubong"* (gifts). Her father's gifts were the biggest secret she ever kept from Grandma Liling. As a little girl, she recalled, Grandma Liling firmly warning her that if she ever bought anything for her father, that she would take her own life. Grandma Liling could never find it in her heart to forgive Grandpa Ramsey for raping her and for the constant abuse that the kids suffered at his hands. My mother was now preparing to enter one of the largest legal cases on record in the history of San Carlos City Municipal Court. Upon arriving in San Carlos City, my mother went straight to Grandma Liling's house to surprise all of us. After all the hugs and kisses, she then sat down with all of us to explain why she was in town. Not just to visit us but to bring justice to a very dark past. Grandma Liling then told us, the kids, to go upstairs and get ready for bed. As soon as we left the adults in the living room, my mother then proceeded to express her quest for revenge towards her father and Mrs. Ramsey. Grandma Liling and Lolo Doming did not know how to respond to her emotional state. They were both quiet and stunned when she told them that she was going to file charges against Grandpa Ramsey in court. Grandma Liling, then said, *"Day! Ayaw na lang kay tiguyang naman silang pareho. Masuko unya ang Ginoo. Sige na lang Day. Wala naman sila na manghilabot."* (Girl! You don't have to do it anymore because they are both old. God might get mad. It is okay girl. They no longer bother us). My mother just gave them that intense look in an angry voice said, *"Ma! Dili gud nako makalimutan ang atong pag-antos dahil sa ilang gihimo. Naka hibao man ang Ginoo ba! Mao man ning gusto sa Ginoo na akong himuon! Para dili na nako sila mahuna hunaon pa!"* (Ma! I could never forget the suffering that we endured because of them. God knows about this! This is what God wanted me to do! So, I would never think of them again).

On the following day, my mother went to the district office of the municipal court to schedule a deportation hearing against her father. The incumbent judge examined the charges presented to him and questioned my mother on why she felt her father, Mr. Ramsey needed to be in a trial or hearing. The presiding judge was also bewildered while reading the signed sealed document from Senator Ferdinand Marcos, specifying the legality of deportation process against Mr. Ramsey. The judge was in disbelief of the accusations because Grandpa Ramsey had always been a highly respected man in the community. He again questioned my mother's convictions to pursue the charges against Mr. Ramsey. All she could say was, "Yes Sir!" The judge now had no choice but to schedule a hearing date. The news regarding an upcoming legal battle circulated quickly throughout the city. When the news reached one of the local Catholic priests about Mr. Ramsey's legal deportation hearing, he immediately traveled to Grandma Liling's house to personally visit my mother. He wanted to talk to my mother in hopes of convincing her to drop the case. As soon as he arrived at Grandma Liling's house, he right away requested to have a private conversation with my mother. He anxiously wanted to disclose to my mother on what Grandpa Ramsey had been praying for and confessing to him for the past twenty years. Father (the priest) knew in the Roman Catholic Church, the Seal of Confession is absolute duty of priests not to disclose anything that they learned from penitents, but in this situation, it was needed to be told. My mother then asked everyone to let them talk privately. The priest then said, *"Elizabeth! Na a koy e bahin nimo na gi kumpisal ni Papa nimo nako pila katuig na hantud karon. Pasay lua lang ko Ginoo intawon kay dili man ma ayo ang akong himuon kay dili man maayo na isulti ang kumpisal nang usa katao. Unya kay lain man na kaso ni kay maka tabang sa kinabuhi nang usa ka tao. Ang Papa nimo ang iyaha gyud na perming ipa ngayo sa Ginoo ay ang imong pag pasaylo sa lahat na iyahang nahimo nimo, sa imong inahan ug imong igsuon. Mahal na mahal ka ni papa nimo. Ang iyaha gyud na gipayao perme sa Ginoo ay ang inyong pagpasaylo niya lalo na "Ikaw! Elizabeth!"* (Elizabeth! I have something to share with you regarding your father's confession all these years up to now. I am going to ask God to forgive me for what I'm ready to do because I'm not supposed to reveal anyone's confession. But this is totally a different case because I would be able to save someone's life. Your Papa always asked God for forgiveness for what he had done to you, your mother, and your brother. Your father loves you very much. He was always hoping that all of you will forgive him especially you, Elizabeth!) He always said, *"Gusto nakong maka estorya ang anak kong si Elizabeth."* (I wanted to talk to my daughter, Elizabeth.) He said that sometimes, Grandpa Ramsey would go to church with teary eyes but never said a word, and then he would just collapse and not breathe for several seconds. These scary incidents happened very often. My mother then responded to Father, *"Wala pa nako makit e ang akong Papa na muhilak"* (I have never seen my father cry.) The priest wanted to express to my mother that her father was very sincere about his confession and it took a lot of great courage to be willing to come forward by asking God first for forgiveness and from everyone he had ever hurt. It was his way of trying to heal his soul and to release all the hatred out of his heart. It's a self-conviction that it is never too late to ask for forgiveness and what a joy it is to receive it. My mother was completely silent and then asked Father to forgive her because this is the only way she could release all her hatred out of her heart, to give her mother justice, and be able to move on with their lives. My mother then said, *"Father! Ipa ngadgi ko sa Ginoo na iyaha kong pasayluon sa akong himuon."* (Father! Please pray for me that God will forgive me for what I'm about to do). Even after the priest's persuasion, my mother continued to pursue her family dispute case against Grandpa Ramsey. In the meantime, Grandpa Ramsey had now been served by the court.

The trial day had now come, Grandpa Ramsey was escorted by the policemen into the courthouse. While my mother was getting ready, she told her mother, Liling, *"Dinhi lang ka Ma! Ayaw gyud pag adto sa munisipyo! Para dili mu taas ang imong dugo! Makapatay unya ka."* (Stay here Ma! Do not go to the municipal! So, that your blood pressure would not go up! You might kill someone). My mother was ready for battle, arrived at the courthouse, while Grandpa Ramsey and Mrs. Ramsey were quietly waiting at the tribunal chairs. The court was now in session, the judge began questioning my mother; *"Ngano mang na a ta dinhi karon? Ngano man na may kaso na inbestigashon batok Mr. Ramsey? Unsa man ang problema na papulion man si Mr. Ramsey sa America? Karon puede ka na Elizabeth musulti."* (Why are we here? Why is there an investigation case against Mr. Ramsey? What is the problem? Why do we have to deport Mr. Ramsey to the United States? Now Elizabeth we are ready to hear your testimony.) Anxious, Elizabeth then started her testimony before the judge with her story beginning when she was only two years old. She explained in detail everything that her father had done to her mother beginning with the first time he raped her at the age of thirteen, and all the punishment and the suffering that she and her brother, Federico, endured while living with him, Mrs. Ramsey and their children. The judge commented, *"Elizabeth, nahinumdom ka gayud sa tanan nga nahitabo kanimo sukad nga ikaw duha ka tuig? Kini talagsaon kaayo."* (Elizabeth, you actually really remembered everything that happened to you since you were two years old? This is very unusual.) "Yes, your honor," my mother, replied. Then the judge said, *"Makaiikag nga hinumdoman nimo ang imong pagkabata."* (It's fascinating that you have a vivid memory of your childhood.) My mother then continued telling her story and all of a sudden, her story got so intense that she started cursing, *"Putang ina mo! pina kaputa ka na sa tanang putang na kit an nako sa tanang kalibutan!"* (Mother fucker! You are the biggest hore that I have seen in the whole world), then she pointed her fingers towards Mrs. Ramsey. Before my mother could curse again, the judge struck his gavel and gave her the warning that he would not allow obscenities in his courtroom. The judge asked my mother, *"Nganong daghan kaayo ang pagdumot ni Mrs. Ramsey?"* (Why there was so much hatred towards your father's wife, Mrs. Ramsey?) My mother was so candid with her story especially when she recalled one of her most painful experiences. The recollected incident was when Mrs. Ramsey minced multiple chili peppers and stuffed all of them in her vagina. She could not forgive and forget Mrs. Ramsey's cruel treatment and other severe verbal and physical punishments that she and her brother, Federico, had been given. She then confessed to the judge that at the age of four years old, she constantly was dreaming of killing Mrs. Ramsey. She told her brother, Federico, that she had a perfect plot to kill Mrs. Ramsey. She then told Federico, this is how it should go: *"Pag matuog na gani siya, ako siyang dunggabon sa kutsilyo!"* (When Mrs. Ramsey goes to sleep, that is when I will stab her with a knife). The dream continued until she was seven years old. The plot to kill Mrs. Ramsey never happened because, luckily, they were both sent back to their mother's house. She thanked God every day that the dreamed up of a murder plot never happened. Before my mother concluded her story, she started pacing up and down towards the policeman. She then reached for his gun from his holster with the intention to kill her father and Mrs. Ramsey. Everyone in the courtroom started screaming and crying out loud because my mother was being held down by the policeman. This was when the judge stopped the hearing and said, *"Igo na ang igo! Nadungog ko ang tanang mga butang. Kini mao ang siguradong ang usa ka sugilanon sa pag-abuso sa gahom ug kaayo talamayong pagtambal ngadto sa mga anak. Ako siguradong kaayo gibati sa imong kasakit ug pag-antos, Elizabeth."* (Enough is enough! I heard everything. This was definitely a story of abuse of power and very despicable treatment towards children. I tremendously felt your pain and suffering, Elizabeth.) All this time, Grandpa Ramsey and Mrs. Ramsey were completely silent and sat still with stone faces and teary eyes full of remorse. The judge then ordered my mother to calm down and have a seat. The judge agreed with my mother that their actions constituted an offense punishable by law. But considering their ages and health, it was not feasible to hand over a verdict. The judge then pleaded with my mother to find forgiveness in her heart not to deport her father, Mr. Ramsey and reconcile with his wife, Mrs. Ramsey. Your father, Mr. Ramsey was too old to be deported. Please allow him to spend the remaining days of his life in San Carlos City. Despite his personal and moral degradation, according to your testimony, he contributed tremendous resources to our city's industry. While the judge was deliberating, Grandpa Ramsey and Mrs. Ramsey kept both of their heads down and continued weeping. After all the deliberations, the presiding judge said, *"Elizabeth, mahimo bang ma pasaylo na nimo ang imong amahan ug ang imong lakang na inahan. Bisag unsaon, amahan gihapon ni mo siya."* (Elizabeth, could you please forgive your father and step-mother. Whatever happened, he is still your father.) The judge continued, *"Siya kanunay sa pagdala sa usa ka bug-at nga palas-anon, ug magatu-aw remorsefully alang sa tanan nga iyang gibuhat kanimo, ang imong inahan ug ang imong mga igsoon nga lalake."* (*H*e would always carry a heavy burden and cry remorsefully for everything he had done to you, your mother and your brother.) This was the moment that when my mother thought long and hard about what the judge and the previous priest had said. The judge then ordered a recess, to give my mother a chance to clear her thoughts. After hours of deliberation and the thirty-minute recess, finally, my mother came to the decision to dismiss the case against her father, Mr. Ramsey and to cancel the deportation process. Her concluding remark was: *"Puede nakong mapa saylo ang akong amahan pero dili gyud nako pasaylo ang babae na yan!"* (I could forgive my father but I could not forgive that woman). My mother's disgusted feelings towards Mrs. Ramsey were still fresh enough in her mind to not forgive and forget. She needed healing to give her strength to move forward on the path that God had laid out for her. In conclusion, the judge addressed, on the record as the closing statement, he congratulated my mother for her change of heart, and wished her good luck, God's blessings, and reconciliation with her family. *"Ako, ang maghuhukom, sa pagpangita sa sinumbong, Mr. Ramsey, dili sad-an sa tanan nga mga kaso. Ikaw gipapauli tanan! Ang korte ang giuswag niya karon! "* (I, the judge, find the defendant, Mr. Ramsey, not guilty of all charges. You are all dismissed! The court is now adjourned!)

The following days after that grueling event, before heading back to Manila, my mother secretly went to church and asked the priest what day and time her father normally goes to church. On the day, while Grandpa Ramsey was praying inside the church, my mother tapped him on his shoulder and whispered that she wanted to speak with him privately. He was so surprised that she was even talking to him. Because of his excitement, he quickly stood up, walked a little faster, as he was eagerly anxious to spend time with his daughter. My mother asked the priest if it was possible to use his office for a private meeting with her father. The priest then allowed them to use his office to conduct their private talk. When the office door closed, Grandpa Ramsey gave his daughter, Elizabeth, a very heartfelt bear hug to show his deepest fatherly love to her and hoped for her forgiveness. They both had been longing for this moment to come. Before she gave him the gifts, she said, *"Pa! kini mao ang tinuod nga mapintas nga sa imong gibuhat kanamo, kay Mama Liling, ug Federico. Kon makapasaylo ang Dios sa atong mga sala, nga ako nga ako dili mopasaylo kaninyo. Kini mao ang bahin sa panahon alang kanako sa pagpasaylo kanimo. Kini nga mga gasa nga akong ihatag kaninyo, gipalit ko kini gikan sa usa sa mga dapit diin ako miawit. Nasayud ko nga gusto ninyo ako sa paghuman sa eskwelahan apan ang tanan gusto ko nga mao sa pag-awit. Akong hunahuna kini mahimo nga ang katapusan nga higayon nga kita makahimo sa pagtan-aw sa usag usa pag-usab. Dad-a sa pag-atiman sa imong kaugalingon."* (Pa! it was really cruel what you did to us, Mama Liling, and Federico. If God can forgive our sins, who am I that I can't forgive you. It is about time for me to forgive you. These gifts that I am going to give you, I bought it from one of the places where I sang. I know that you wanted me to finish school but all I wanted was to sing. I think this may be the last time that we would be able to see each other again. Take care of yourself). She gave him another hug for the last time and said goodbye. She left Grandpa Ramsey, standing alone, crying remorsefully, and felt so fragile that he had to sit down. All he could do was to watch her walk away from him.

After my mother has completed her monumental accomplishment that she needed to do in San Carlos City, she then left the following day back to the city of Manila. She then decided not to go back to Mr. Marcos office to let him know the outcome of the case. She did not have the courage to tell him that she had a change of heart and dismissed the case. When she had her moment of silence, she thanked God for giving her the strength, to forget her hurt feelings, and to extend the grace of forgiveness, so she could give herself the gift of grudge-free living and be able to move on with her life:

From God's Word
"Clothe yourselves with compassion, kindness, humility, gentleness, and patience. Bear with each other and forgive whatever grievances you may have against one another. Forgive as the Lord forgave you." (Colossians 3:12-13)

In the year of 1966, my brother, Isaac Jr., at the age of fourteen, moved in with my mother in Manila, while my sister, Mary Ann, and I stayed in San Carlos City to be cared for by Grandma Liling and Lolo Doming. All these years, the diagnosis of Grandma Liling's illness was still unknown to my mother, and Lolo Doming. Grandma Liling asked her daughter, Elizabeth, if she could send her seven pesos to purchase a house which was formerly owned by uncle Federico's mother-in-law. What had happened was uncle Federico's mother-in-law filed bankruptcy which left her no choice but to sell the house. It was a very good deal at that time, so my mother told Grandma Liling that she would send her the money in two days. My grandma, finally fulfilled her dream to have her own house even though the land was owned by the Caballeros. It did not take a long time for my mother to pay off the house while continued paying rent for the land.

Years passed by, Grandma Liling became very ill to the point that she was so weak and fragile. Her pain was so unbearable, that it was even impossible for her to walk around the house. One bright sunny day, Grandma Liling asked me to talk to Lolo Doming to go to church and request a priest for a home visit for her to receive a Sacrament of the Anointing of the Sick. Besides the blessing, she also wanted the priest to bless her blissful relationship with Lolo Doming by performing a marriage ceremony before God called her home. Days passed by after their marriage was blessed in 1971, unfortunately, Grandma Liling died of an unknown illness.

Upon Grandma Liling's death, my mother came home to San Carlos City to arrange the funeral. After all these years, no one in our family knows what the cause of Grandma Liling's death was. After the funeral, my mother asked her brother, Federico, to have a temporary full custody of Mary Ann and me while we were finishing at the elementary grades school. Our house was then occupied by my uncle Federico's family. Presently, on said date, the property was no longer occupied by Ramsey's family.

Years later, my mother decided to relinquish ownership of the property because it brought back too many bad memories that constantly lingered in the back of her mind about Grandma Liling's health conditions while living in that house. One of the difficult memories, when her mother, Liling, was not able to breathe, she ran into the balcony to gasp for air so she could breathe again. She did not want those painful memories to haunt her forever. She was also rationalizing the situation that eventually none of her children would ever go back to San Carlos City to permanently settle down. It was in the best interest of her to give up the ownership and passed it on to her brother, Federico's, family. After my sister, Mary Ann, and I graduated from elementary, my uncle Federico escorted us on very long days of ship ride all the way to the city of Manila. My mother's driver picked us up from the pier. As soon as we arrived at the house, we were so surprised to meet a two-year-old sister named, Maria Luisa. As I recalled, the last time I was visited by my mother, her story was that her belly was big because she had a tumor. Per her explanation, the doctor determined that the medical diagnosis collected from the hospital x-ray and combined with another testing that had been performed, that it was a benign tumor rapidly growing and that needed to be operated on and removed or it would kill her. On the day of the surgery, the doctor was shocked to discover that the tumor turned out to be a baby. He saw a baby's butt and feet sticking out from the vaginal canal. He had to swiftly make a drastic decision to perform a caesarian section to deliver the baby girl. Since it was a premature delivery, the baby had to be kept in an incubator for another four months to keep her alive.

Federico had nine children – in the picture, it's Federico with some of his children including Mary Ann and me.

My Uncle Federico, like his sister Elizabeth, loved to sing and perform in different fiestas. He worked at the San Carlos City Sugar Milling Company during his lifetime. On Christmas day, he then transformed himself as the Santa Claus for the Sugar Milling Company housing community. Uncle Federico had nine children with his wife, Angelita Corbita, asked my mother to help raise some of their children. Sadly, Uncle Federico died on March 20, 1979. After the demise of my Uncle Federico, my mother kept her promise to take good care of his family by raising five of his children in Manila and sent them all to school. When they became older, they left her house to start their own lives.

STARDOM & ACCOMPLISHMENTS

With the grace of God, my mother, Elizabeth Ramsey made it to stardom. She became a famous singer, comedian and an actress which made her an all-around entertainer. Her performances captivated the Philippine audiences as well as her shows in the United States. She took her singing career seriously and worked very hard to maintain her popularity for more than five decades. She was strongly disciplined when it came to her performances, even to the point that she would give 100% regardless of whether she got paid or not - she never let her audiences down. The longevity of her showbiz career, which spanned over fifty-six years, summed up her versatility, unique talent, personality, and love for humanity. She earned widespread recognition and numerous awards for her live performances and movies. She was a true innovator and had never been duplicated. With all her accomplishments, some of the most memorable moments were her performances from the following: U.S. Military bases in the Philippines, American Military facilities fighting in the Vietnam War, Philippine and U.S. Veterans Affairs and Administrations, Philippine U.S. Embassy, religious and non-religious fund-raising events, even in rigid mountains of Mindanao Island where many of the entertainers never dared to perform. She became one of the most successful female performers on live shows, TV, and movies. Her one regret in her life was that she did not expand her musical recording talent. She only had two original songs recorded by Crystal recording: one was a Visayan song entitled "Masyaw" and a Tagalog song entitled "Magapatuka Na Lang Ako Sa Ahas". The tagalog song became her trademark when the song was used as the theme song of the Superwheel commercial. She eventually formed her own band and dance group which I have been involved in and was named the Elizabeth Ramsey Dance Group.

Elizabeth Ramsey Dance Group

My fascinating mother built her career through live performances and became the most successful female Rock 'N' Roll artist in the Philippines. She risked her life for the cause of bringing joy and happiness to those who needed it which summed up some of the incidents that happened to her in the following:

- ❖ It all started when she was 15 or 16 years old, campaigning for politicians in San Carlos City when the truck she was riding fell off from a mountain curve but miraculously she survived. The accident cracked and bundled up all the bones in her knees. The doctor did not reconstruct the bones in her knees back to their original positions. This accident did not stop her from going back out on stage to deliver an electrifying Rock N' Roll performance.

❖ When she performed for the U.S. military troops in the Vietnam War, she contracted malaria (intermittent and remittent fever caused by a protozoan parasite that invades the red blood cells.) This was transmitted by the mosquitoes in the jungle warfare of Vietnam. The symptoms that she suffered, such as loss of blood, were so severe that she required a blood transfusion to level her red blood cells. The producer was ready to send her back home to the Philippines but knowing her fighting spirit, she strongly insisted on performing wherever her entertainment services were badly needed until her engagement contract ended. She was a true trooper because, for her, nothing was more fulfilling than bringing enjoyment to others.

❖ On one occasion in Mindanao, my mother's sugar level reached an alarming rate of 500, and twice, her sugar level dropped down to zero. Everybody was terrified at that moment and thought she was pronounced dead. When the doctor examined her, he was astonished at how she was able to survive and able to continue her hardcore live performance after these critical medical conditions of her sugar level. These incidents happened countless times in her lifetime. But because of her devotion to Santo Niño, she survived.

For five decades, she established a successful career in both movies and television. She was known not only for her singing but also for her wit and comedic style. Her style in comedy was not an imitation but an original act based on her life experiences, and facts about other people's lives by telling it like it is. Here is the list of her movies, television, radio and live shows:

- 2010 Diva   **TV**/Comedy/Musical

- 2008 Dyesebel   TV Adventure
- 1997 Strict Ang Parents ko   **Movie** Comedy
- 1996 Neber 2-Geder   **Movie** Comedy
- 1996 Hindi Ako Ander   **Movie** Comedy
- 1996 SPO1 Don Juan: Da
  Dancing Policeman   **Movie** Comedy
- 1980 Reyna Ng Pitong Gatang   **Movie** Comedy
- 1976 Barok   **Movie** Comedy
- 1973 Ato Ti Bondying   **Movie** Comedy
- 1972 Trubador   **Movie** Fantasy
- 1972 Sa Jeepney Ang Hirap Sa
  Goodtime Ang Sarap   **Movie** Comedy
- 1972 Pearly Shells   **Movie** Musical
- 1970 Areglado, Boss   **Movie** Action
- 1969 The Musical Giant   **Musical**
- 1964 Petrang Paminta   **Movie** Comedy
- 1964 Mga Guerrera   **Movie** Comedy
- 1964 Eddie Long Legs   **Movie** Comedy
- 1964 Pinoy Beatles   **Movie** Musical
- 1964 Jukebox Jamboree   **Movie** Comedy
- 1964 Let's Go   **Movie** Comedy
- 1964 Mga Kanang Kamay   **Movie** Comedy
- 1963 Ang Bukas Ay Akin   **Movie** Drama
- 1963 Pinakamalaking Takas   **Movie** Comedy
- 1962 InThis Corner   **Movie** Action
- 1962 Pitong Atsay   **Movie** Comedy
- 1960 Prinsesa Naranja   **Movie** Romantic
- 1960 Beatnik   **Movie** Comedy
- 1959 Ipinagbili Kami Ng Aming
  Tatay   **Movie** Comedy
- 1958 Ang Lo'Waist Gang at Si
  Og Sa Mindoro   **Movie** Comedy

- 1958 Mga Liham Kay Tiya Dely   **Radio** (3rd Segment Story)

Elizabeth Ramsey Signature Movie
Prinsesa Naranja

ANG BUKAS AY AKIN was the movie that Elizabeth Ramsey got nominated for Best Supporting Actress at the FAMAS Award – 1964

RAMSEY'S COLLAGE OF ELIZABETH MOVIES, MUSICAL, RADIO, SHOWS POSTERS

IT'S THE BIGGEST BARGAIN ... IN LAUGHS!
DOLPHY
IPINAGBILI KAMI NG AMING TATAY

GET HEP TO THIS OFF-BEAT PIC
COME YE AND SHAKE WITH THE...
BeATNiK
dolphy - eddie arenas
susan roces - jose mari
the wing duo
panchito alba - rod navarro
pacita arana - meldy corrale
nori dalisay - eddie gutierre
lito legaspi -
boy alano -
mitos seva -
tony cayado
dolphy & nikki
jose leonardo
luciano b. carlos
carding cruz
DALISAY... JANUARY 20-29

DALISAY PICTURES, INC.
Presents
THE NAUGHTY, NUTTY MISADVENTURES OF 7 ZANY HOUSEMAIDS... THEIR LIVES AND LOVES (SORT OF) BOTH IN THEIR GUARDED AND UNGUARDED MOMENTS...!
CHICHAY
ARURAY
DELY ATAY-ATAYAN
ELIZABETH RAMSEY
MENGAY
PATSY
METRING DAVID
PITONG ATSAY
STARRING:
HECTOR REYES • ZENY BUENA
INTRODUCING
AURORA ORTIZ
Co-Starring:
CARIDAD SANCHEZ
NIEVES MANUEL
MIGUEL LOPEZ
RAFAEL JIMENEZ
Screenplay:
GREG MACABENTA
Video 48
Featuring:
KULAS KALTAS
TINTOY • POPOY
DALISAY • MARCH 30
STORY & DIRECTION:
TONY SANTOS

WANTED! 7 MOST DANGEROUS CHARACTERS ON THE LOOSE.... THEY'RE OUT TO CRACK YOUR FUNNY-BONES TO PIECES!
711013
771169
110137
691107
713961
131313
676869
PATSY • DELY • CHICHAY • ARURAY • ELIZABETH • MENGGAY • METRING
ATAYATAYAN
RAMSEY
DAVID
PiNAKAMALAKiNG TAKAS
(NG 7 ATSAY)
STARRING:
JOSE MARI ★ JEAN LOPEZ
FEATURING:
BOY GARCIA
VENCHITO GALVEZ
WITH THE SPECIAL PARTICIPATION OF
JOSE DE VILLA
TONY SANTOS
SUPPORTED BY:
CLARA YUMUL
Video 48
TONY CAMONTE
MUSIC:
NESTOR ROBLES
TONY SANTOS
SOON at LIFE THEATRE

CENTER OPENS FEB. 28
BOB SOLER
RODOLFO CRISTOBAL
BERT SILVA
JERRY PONS
TONY CRUZ Jr.
JOE de CASTRO
and CARLOS PADILLA Jr.
"mga Kanang Kamay"
STARRING
ELIZABETH RAMSEY · JOSE VERGARA
VINCE JUAREZ · FLOR BIEN
BOY PINEDA · CONCHITA CRUZ
ROSAURO ORACION
INTRODUCING SEVEN COEDS
CHIQUI SOMES
NINA ZALDUA · DULCE LUKBAN · MARGIE TANQUINTIC
SUZZETTE SPEIS · JOJI CRESPO · MERLE HUGGINS
STORY PABLO SANTIAGO
SCREENPLAY JOSE C. GARCIA
MUSIC TONY MAIQUEZ
DIRECTION TONY SANTOS

GLOBE Theatre – April 10 to 19
PROUDLY PRESENTS
Eddie Mesa * Jose Mari
Helen Gamboa * Vilma Valera
Reycard Duet * Elizabeth Ramsey
Chiqui Somes AND Jerry Pons
GLOBE THEATRE
APRIL 10 - 19
BAGUIO CITY
LET'S GO
"Let's GO"
STARRING
BOY FRANCISCO - JOE DE CASTRO
SAMMY BARRETTO - JOSE GARCIA - PONGA
BOY PINEDA - DULCE LUKBAN
MARGIE TANQUINTIC · SUZZETTE SPEIS
FEATURING
ELECTROMANIAC - HI JACKS
PAQUITO TOLEDO
TOMMY C. DAVID
DIRECTION PABLO SANTIAGO

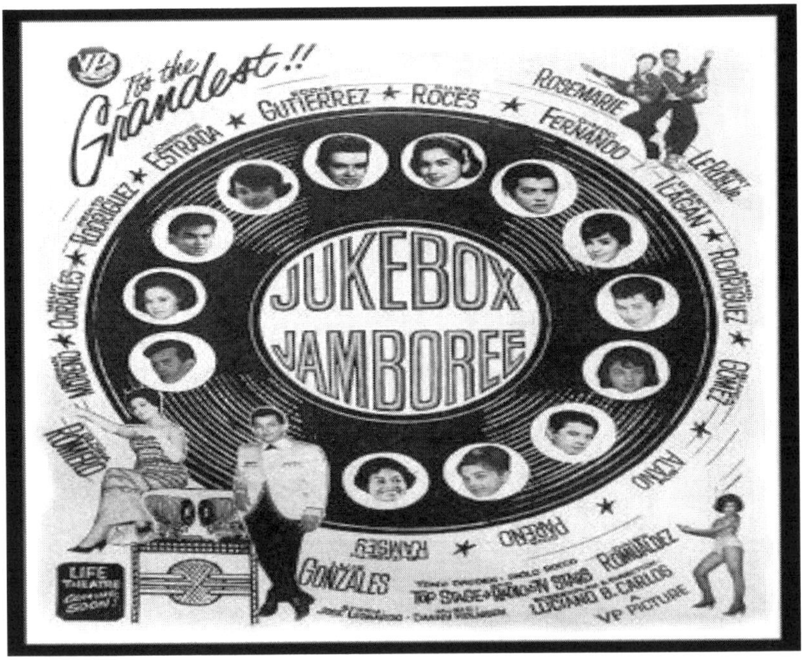

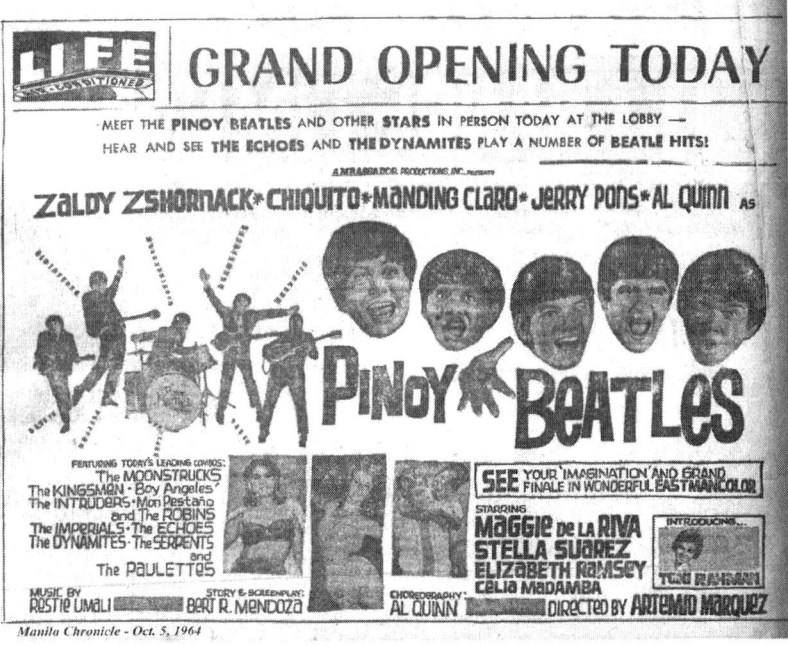

Manila Chronicle - Oct. 5, 1964

108

SO YOUNG... SO INNOCENT... FIGHTING FOR FREEDOM!
AMBASSADOR PRODUCTIONS, INC. PRESENTS
MIRIAM JURADO
ZENY ZABALA
EVA DARREN
ALONA ALEGRE
CARINA MOJER
TONI RAHMAN
ELIZABETH RAMSEY
AND MAGGIE DE LA RIVA
MGA GUERRERA
STARRING
EDDIE RODRIGUEZ FAMAS BEST ACTOR 1963 ABE TUGAK
ANDY GARCHITORENA · EDDIE TORRENTE · LIMBO LAGDAMEO
TOMMY ROMULO · RUBEN RAMOS · TONY VILLAR AND
CARLOS PADILLA, JR. IN A SPECIAL ROLE JOSE PADILLA, JR.
MUSIC BY TONY MAIQUEZ · STORY & SCREENPLAY: BEN FELEO · DIRECTED BY SOL GAUDITE · OPENS AT LIFE -- NOVEMBER 4

JBC PRODUCTIONS PROUDLY PRESENTS
THE BIGGEST STAR EVER TO HIT THE SCREEN
IKE LOZADA
LINDA MARTIN
MISS CIELITO DEL MUNDO
FEATURING:
PERLA ADEA
AND BOBET TORRES
STARRING:
BEN DAVID
BETTY MENDEZ
TOMMY ANGELES
METRING DAVID
PROSPERO LUNA
RIC M. DELA ROSA
TOM CALMA
AND TONY SANTOS, JR.
AND THE SPECIAL PERFORMANCE OF
ROGER CALVIN
(COURTESY OF LEA PRODUCTIONS)
PLUS THE PHILIPPINES TOP SINGERS
ELIZABETH RAMSEY
RUBEN TAGALOG
RIC MANRIQUE, JR.
PAULINE SEVILLA
SUSAN LA TORRE
ROMY MALLARI
HELEN VELA
BLINKERS COMBO
AND
MISS DIANA CRUZ
THE MUSICAL GIANT
SPECIAL PARTICIPATIONS: JOHNNY MIDNIGHT · MELY FACTORA
EDDIE 'DWOW' ILAGAN · VIC MORALES · CRIS DALUZ · HENRY RAGAS
GUEST STARS
HERMAN MORENO AND THE Musical TEEN-AGE IDOLS
Music by: DEMIT VELASQUEZ · Story by: DAMBUHALANG DJ · Directed by: THE FORGOTTEN DIRECTOR

PRUDENTIAL FILMS INTERNATIONAL PRESENTS
MAGNOLIA FILM PRODUCTIONS
VICTOR WOOD
AURORA SALVE
Pearly Shells
GERALDINE · DARIUS RAZON · AMALIA BRAZA · JACKIE BELMONTE
IN HAWAIIAN COLOR
STARRING:
DELY ATAY-ATAYAN · ELIZABETH RAMSEY · D' BIG '3' SULLIVANS
SPECIAL PARTICIPATION OF TINTOY and JUSTO C. JUSTO
FEATURING: ALICE MENDEZ · INTRODUCING: GEMMA HERNAEZ · AINO VALDES · RICO RIOS
SCREENPLAY: RICO BELLO OMAGAP MUSIC: PEWEN
Director: JOSE 'PEPE' WENCESLAO

EMAR PICTURES PROUDLY PRESENTS
A TOUGH MAN FOR A TOUGH JOB
JOSEPH ESTRADA
AS PEPE
LIVING IT HIGH AND WILD
PILAR PILAPIL
AS PILAR
IN
AREGLADO, BOSS!
JERRY PONS
ELIZABETH RAMSEY
PAG SINABI KONG HINDI, HINDI!
AREGLADO, BOSS! YOU SAID IT!
VIC SILAYAN
ANGELO VENTURA · ROMY DIAZ · AVEL MORADO AND RAMON ZAMORA
GUEST STARS JOSE MORELOS AND CHIQUI SANTOS
MUSIC · ERNANI CUENCO CINEMATOGRAPHY · FRED CONDE WITH THE VOICE OF IKE LOZADA
WRITTEN AND DIRECTED BY AUGUSTO BUENAVENTURA

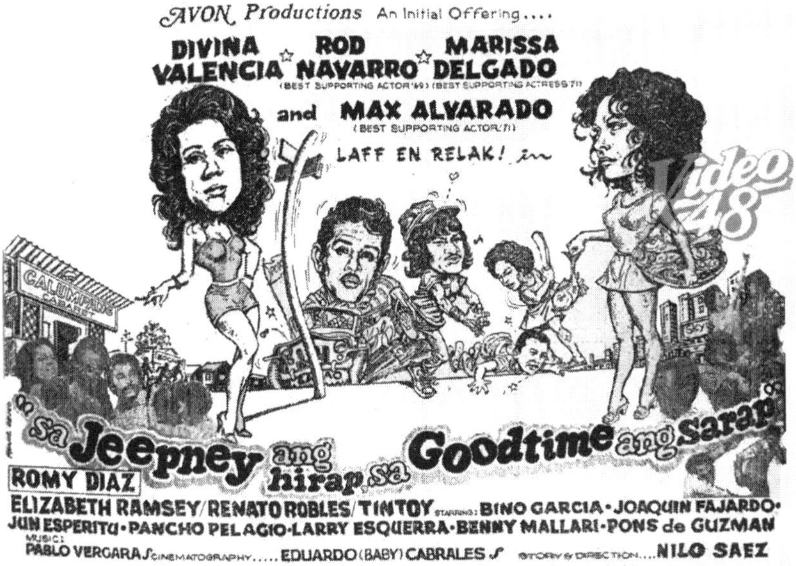

"THE BEST OF BONDYING"

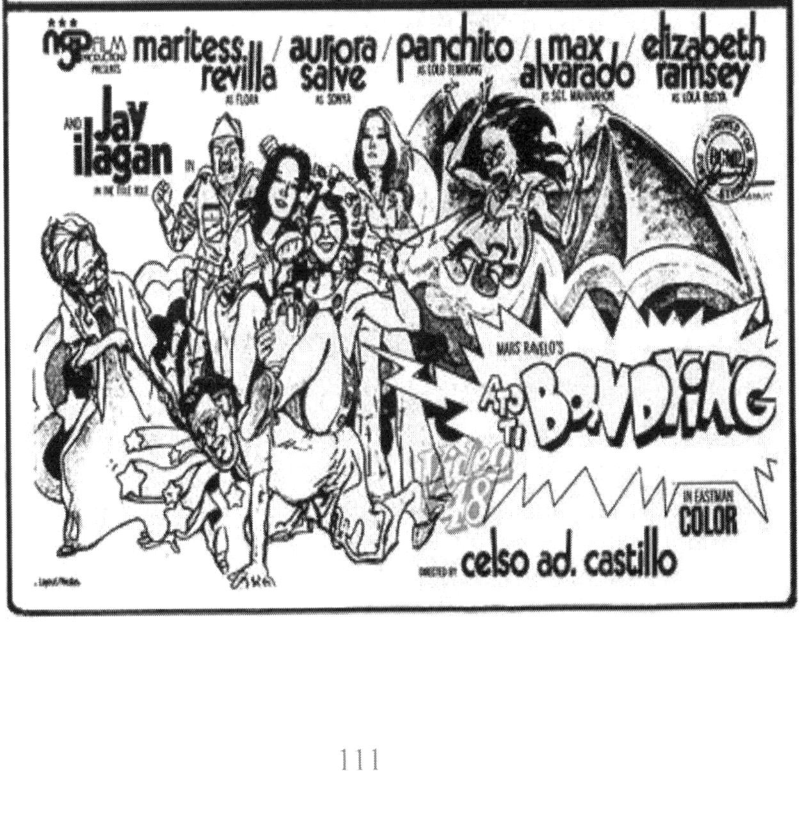

PAMASKO NG
HPS FILM PRODUCTIONS
AT HANDOG PARA SA
1976 Filipino Film Festival
CHIQUITO
TRIXIA GOMEZ
MAX ALVARADO
BAROK
INILATHALA SA HIWAGA KOMIKS
TANGE - JOAQUIN FAJARDO - PALITO - ARLENE SISON
ELY ROQUE - JUN SANTOS - NORMA YUMUL - MANUEL DAGUL
GERMAN MORENO - ELIZABETH RAMSEY - JORGIE QUIZON
DIREKSYON F.H.CONSTANTINO

NORA AUNOR
LLOYD SAMARTINO & ANTHONY ALONZO
BEZ CORTEZ
CHICHAY
ELIZABETH RAMSEY
ENRICO VILLA
IKE LOZADA - GERMAN MORENO
Reyna ng
PITONG GATANG
SPECIAL PARTICIPATIONS OF
ZENY ZABALA
PINKY MONTILLA
INTRODUCING:
TARA FORTEZA
PAUL RAMIREZ
ENRICO VILLA
VIC ANAS
CASTELLANO
DIRECTED BY
MARIA SARET

Amanda Page
Cara M
& Michael de Mesa
Andrew E.
&
Redford White
NEBER 2 GEDER
Ben Feleo

Chiquito
Gary Estrada
Elizabeth Ramsey
Erika Fife
Bernadette Allyson
and
Amanda Page
STRICT ang peyrents ko
Also starring
Danny Pansalin
Zeny Zabala
Alicia Alonzo
Marissa Delgado
Pocholo Montes
Gammy Viray
Michael Gomez
Directed By Edgardo ' Boy ' Vinarao

FUNNY HOUR

This Filipina/Jamaican had been cast as a comedian even though in her heart she was a versatile singer. Her bold, brash and opinionated slapstick comedic style which captivated the Filipino and foreign audiences still reflected her outspoken sensibility. My mother did not mind using foul language, and to get her point across, she amazingly talked about sex, handicaps, as a marriage counselor, or old age and old folks, which led to some graphic images of characters that kept her audiences squirming and laughing out loud simultaneously. To celebrate the funny hour moment with the one and only Ms. Ramsey, here are the handful of her best bits:

☀ "Good Evening" in different languages for our foreign exchange: In Tagalog – *"Magandang gabi po!"* – in Japanese is very different because they always have their heads down and have their legs wide open like sakang (bandy)

– "Isusu ni! Ano ni! Isuksuk ni!" – in Pampanga – "Nasalo ang bola sa titi!" – in Bicol – "Mga uragon kamo!" – in Visayan – "Maayong gabi-i sa inyong tanan, pesting yawa!" – in Ilocano, I have to be careful because of President Marcos and Mr. Joe Quirino, whom I co-hosted on his TV show for two years. Mr. Joe Quirino taught me how to say good evening in Ilocano – "maimbag sa gabi-i na naiyot sa amin!"

☼ Ladies! Do not be afraid when you are 50 years old to wear a mini dress. Look at me! I had been wearing a short dress in the Philippines all these years and nothing ever happened to me.

☼ Imagine in the Philippines, this is a true story – I went to Tondo and it was so dark, and you know there are lots of gangs there: oxo-oxo, sige-sige, bala-bala. Remember what your parents said, "Children! It's very dark over there, ha! 10 o'clock, you better come home! Do not pass that place because it's very dark!" "Ma de desgrasya kayo!" (You will have accident). Hindi ko alam ang disgrasya sa English, (I don't know what is disgrasya in English?) Ah! I know now! "disgrace!" I have to allow myself – I have to walk down there just in case I get lucky and have disgrace at the age of 75. Always looking for the "disgrace" all the way to Arizona "dissirt!" (desert)

☼ You know! "mahirap" (hard) when your singing too high! My ovary goes down! Why are you laughing? I'm 75 but I still have my ovary! Loco! (crazy!) "You!" You want to try me!

☀ I want people to know who I am in this world. My mother was a Filipina/Spanish – beautiful woman! – my father –never mind! – really my father is from Kingston, Jamaica – when my mother delivered me – it was really a sad story because you see when a woman delivers a baby, the doctor will slap the baby's butt, so the baby can breathe – but this time, the doctor did not slap me – he slapped my mother – I don't blame the doctor because the doctor was expecting something will come out nice. He said, "Hoy! babae! Sa susunod huwag kang manganak dito sa hospital nang isang unggoy!" (Hey! Woman! Next time don't give birth in the hospital with a monkey!)

☀ Ma! When I was a baby, you know when "sumu suso ang bata" (baby is breastfed) – everytime my face turned left – my mom turned her head to the right and if I turn my face to the right – she turned her head to the left – so I asked her - you tried not to look at me but it was okay – you are lucky to have a baby like me! I was in the Clover Theater and became Elizabeth Ramsey – look at me! – If I'm beautiful now, I will be the number one prostitute in the world.

☀ I told my mother, you know mom, just tell me if you really are my mother? I will not be offended, you know mom because I'm the only one working, and I am the survivor. I'm the mother and the father of my children. It's okay with me. If I'm an adopted child! My mother was so angry with me – "Hayop ka! - kung magsalita ka, pesting yawa! Para kang hari – hindi mo ba alam – animal ka – napakahirap mag pa suso nang unggoy!" (Animal you! – The way you talk, bull shit! You think you're a king – don't you know – animal you – it is not easy to breastfeed a monkey!)

☀ Someone asked me if I celebrate my birthday. I told him, I don't celebrate my birthday – he kept asking me, where is the party? What party? I'm not a liberal party, I'm a socialista party!

☀ Someone asked me, Ms. Ramsey, what is your secret for looking young. I have gray hair and you still look the same. Elizabeth said I don't know maybe because "I only take a bath once a month and no sex!"

☀ Ladies and gentlemen – sometimes I have to speak Tagalog because my English is not favorable to me – even I keep opening and closing my legs, still, nothing happens!

☀ German Moreno told me that I am a legend – means ancestors! I told him – I'm not a legend because I was with Jose Rizal but not with General McArthur!

☀ German Moreno asked me to call him kuya Germs. I told him I don't want to call you kuya Germs because I don't want to have germs in my body!

☀ An audience asked: Mama Beth, I just want to ask you, Mama Beth, what beauty secret you're using. Can you give us some tips? Elizabeth replied, beauty secret! What do you think of me, Pilita Corrales? Are you crazy? Up to now, there are still lots of crazy people. People talk about cancer – my face is my cancer! "Buang!" (Crazy!)

MEMORABLE MOMENTS

During my mother's, early years, she was a chain smoker. A carton of cigarettes a week was one of her stress releases. In the early 50's, cigarette smoking was very popular and perceived as being a cool cat. Subsequently, the smoking habit caused her high blood pressure to accelerate. Her smoking affected her singing voice from the higher range to baritone. She attempted to stop smoking multiple times but was unsuccessful. When her voice started to get deeper, and it was getting harder for her to sustain her breathing, that was when she decided to quit her smoking habit which, unfortunately, it took her forty years. After her smoking addiction, she was diagnosed having the symptoms of borderline diabetes because she replaced the nicotine with sugary drinks to combat her urge to smoke.

At sixty years old, my mother continued to amaze her audiences with her singing, comedy and her Rock 'N' Roll live performances on the TV, and on location venues. When my mother devoted herself to Santo Niño, she deeply believed that He protected her all the time. She always said, "Santo Niño is on my side!" One of her testimonies was when she went to the doctor to have her lungs checked; the doctor was shocked to discover that there was no trace of scar tissue in her lungs from the long years of her smoking habit.

At the age of 82, my mother continued to dazzle her audiences with her entertaining abilities. Her fans, family, and friends had wondered why she did not have any wrinkles on her face and body. My mother would simply give credit to Santo Niño saying "He made me look this way." She collected over two hundred statues and images of Santo Niño, besides statues and images of the Blessed Mother, God the Father, and other Catholic Saints. All these statues and images became part of her devotion and faith.

**She would plainly say:
"That's the mysterious part of my life."**

ELIZABETH AND HER CHILDREN

Isaac – the eldest child, Mary Ann – second to the eldest, Susan – third to the eldest, Maria Luisa – the youngest child

Elizabeth became a United States citizen on
August 01, 1998.

These are the unforgettable emotions and show business chronicles that defined the memorable times provided by the following family members, closest friends, and employers. They are offering an inspirational personal address of their association with Ms. Ramsey. "Time is limitless – the only thing that matters is the moment you shared."

Mary Ann Johnson: Second Child

What I remember about a memorable moment with my mother was when I was young, living in San Carlos City, Negros Occidental, she always brings us toys and dolls from Manila. But I never liked playing with dolls, so what I used to do, I take off their body parts. My mother always took care of me all throughout my adulthood. My mother and I have the same hobby, we loved to shop as our way of releasing our stress. She always wants me to do good in life. I love you so much Ma and I missed you a lot. I wish we could have spent more time together. I will forever always love you.

Dyana Ware: Granddaughter

My grandma Elizabeth was a great loving mother and grandmother. She always did her very best for her family to keep them close to each other. She was a very generous and kind spirited grandma who helps those in need and unfortunately, more than herself. I still remember those times when grandma stayed with us in California, and we go to the Filipino market to buy those "balikbayan" boxes and fill them up with food, clothes, watches, and toys to send to the Philippines. She taught me how to appreciate what we have and be grateful for every blessing you receive whether it's big or small. Always be humble and generous to the unfortunate. Grandma was rich in love and had a heart of gold. I will never forget the lessons and wisdom. "Grandma will be forever in my heart." I will always love you, Grandma.

Rodney Ware: Grandson

My grandma Elizabeth was a unique individual. She never worries about money but how she wanted to present herself on stage. She was always herself, very kind and always ready to help anyone in need. People were naturally friend to her. Some say I get my comedic attitude and demeanor from her. I truly believe; I did! I'm like that now, always willing to help someone thanks to Grandma. She always told me to be happy and to stop getting too fat because diabetes ran in our family. She taught me to love myself, forgive myself and to always be there for families. Her legacy lives on through us. I love you Grandma and may continue to watch us from heaven.

Cherrieh Kahlika Pittman: Granddaughter

Wish I knew my grandmother more. Every time I saw her, it was many years apart. She was the matriarch. That much I did know. All of her children, even as adults, frequently sought her counsel. She took my brother Michael and myself in when my own mother couldn't look after us. She was an eccentric woman with a presence that commanded attention where ever she went. I don't think the apple falls far from the tree as her granddaughter. I see some commonalities running from her, through my mother, down to me. We're all very quirky, independent women with gaped front teeth.

Dennis Wadlington: Adopted Son

I'm not sure what year it was when I met Ms. Ramsey but I know it changed my life. Susan and I would have long conversations with her mother, while we watched Youtube videos at home, but I had never seen her perform. I just knew she was a huge celebrity because everywhere Susan and I went with her she would be greeted with kindness and laughter and everyone wanted pictures of her. I thought I was with one of the Beatles sometimes. We took her to a

Seafood Market one day and I swear it was like the scene from the Salina movie where she got mobbed in the mall, every person including the employee's stopped to talk to Mama Beth, it was amazing. I just stood there with a big smile on my face; you could feel the love from everyone. Mama Beth always had the most interesting stories about her life and her family. She loved to cook meals for us. This little tiny lady had been through so much adversity in her life and made it through it all. I would ask her; how did you make it through all of that? Her always answer was "My Santo Niño!" I will always have a special place in my heart for this wonderful woman that came into my life. She always made me smile and laugh, even though I sometimes didn't know what the hell she was saying, she just was funny that way. We didn't have you long enough. Love you, Mama Beth!

Pilita Corrales: Best Friend

There will never be another like her in the world of showbiz. She made millions of people happy with her comedy routines, her songs, her music and her personality. I am so thankful to have been part of her shows. I learned a lot about comedy, just by looking at her. She will really be missed by everyone who saw her perform. Dear Elizabeth, now that you are in heaven please pray for us. Missed you!

Jules Nesenblatt: Family Friend

Elizabeth Ramsey. There's something about that name. That lady you hear about in your local Filipino Community whose legendary Singer and Actress back in the Philippines. No one can top her as she's ahead of her game. Her rumors as a comedian, bold, brash and eclectic for boldly growing out her underarm hair and go as natural to shock society gives her title "Funny Lady." She was an outcast and she enjoyed a life that way. I've learned to become one of her best friends as the instrumental tool that helped coach me in my relationships with family, society, and career. In fact, it was her who helped me grow into my dating relationships (when I was a single mother) that lead to my successful marriage with my husband, Neil. I consider myself blessed to have such opportunities to see her from the inside out of what this amazing woman is made of, which I'm certain only a handful have seen! Elizabeth was a great storyteller, sharing her days of growing up chasing her dream to be on stage. She was passionate, generous to a Fault Lady. I say generous to a Fault because she's willing to give the shirt off her back if she can. I say this because she babysat for my son, Dean when I was in distressed with finding sitters, back in the day. Yes, she was THAT Lady. She was a woman that loved life and enjoyed sharing it even if it leads her into poverty. To me, she was a Down to Earth Cool Mama. My good Friend, a life Coach, dances Buddy, and a Mother figure that blessed me into her family. She was an intelligent lady that grew up in the School of Hard Knocks. Yes! To the rumor that she'll kick your ass in person, as she'll do on stage!

Girlie Bayron: Family Friend

Life on earth is only temporary but along the way we met acquaintances that will become our dear friend, a friend close to our heart, that person is Ms. Elizabeth Ramsey. Sometime in 2001, I met her at the Heart Center and instantly I felt her magic that engraved in my heart until her last days. I watched her at the Music Museum and sent word that I want to meet her personally, that started our close interaction with friends, more than friends and my buddy…with the foundation of LOVE and RESPECT. Another time she requested me to be with her in one of her performances. In the car, Beth was practicing her ad lib script at the same time she was telling me "Inday! Ikaw talaga ang best friend ko!" (Girl! You are really my best friend!) It is an honor hearing her tell me that unexpected endearment. I will cherish those words in my heart now and always. Knowing my relationship with her was greatly appreciated. Never a dull moment with my Buddy and I just love her call of endearment with a loving voice and care. When she got sick, I voluntarily imposed on myself that I'll be with her. Her last days touched my heart, thinking a great Performer also experienced pain, loneliness, and despair going away eternally…so be it. As real performances have curtain call we don't know when. I can say Beth lived to the fullest that made her very dear to her family, close friends and I are one of them, her fans, I salute her endearment. Never look for LOVE, let LOVE find you…and I say never look for friends…loyal, caring, understanding friends will always find you…and I found one with my dear Elizabeth…" Sleep well."

Mryna Francisco – Family Friend

In 1997 is the year when I met Mommy Beth in person. Since that time, we got to see her every Saturday together with my daughter who is sick with cancer to bring flowers for the Santo Niño and Mama Mary in her small altar in their house in Sunnyvale. Rain or shine we always come to offer flowers and prayer for my daughter sickness, and there are times when we do our rosary with her. We can feel that the Mahal Na Santo Niño (loving Senor Santo Niño is present inside her altar and her voice keep changing while she is reciting the holy rosary. Not only that there a time that the spirit of the Mahal Na Santo Niño is with her because she was talking like a kid. Through our prayers, my daughter's cancer did heal. She lived through High school until our Lord called her to be in heaven. Believe it or not, all the things that she is telling us became so real. Whenever we bring some friends with us, Mommy Beth can tell what's going on with your life, etc. That's why they were so surprised about it as if she is a fortune teller. From buying flowers for her altar every

Saturday, shopping at Ross, going to a Tong Kee Noodle House, was our routine whenever she was in California during spring and summer time. She doesn't want to stay during winter time in the US because she hates the cold weather. There is no dull moment when we are with her. Since she can't remember my name nor pronounce it right, she just calls me "Margaret." It was so sad when I heard the news that she passed away in the Philippines. I always try to call her and ask how's she doing and we exchange stories as well. I really miss you so much, Mommy Beth. You will always be in my heart and I know that you are now happy with our Lord. Take care of my daughter over there in heaven and give her a big hug for me. Love you always!

GMA Television Network, Inc.

There will never be another Elizabeth Ramsey in Philippine showbiz. The brand of entertainment that she offered was uniquely her own. Through the years, GMA Network had the pleasure of experiencing Ms. Elizabeth's uncanny talent as she was either featured or appeared as a guest in some of our TV programs including the variety show Student Canteen (where she joined in a singing contest in 1958), comedy program Lagot Ka, Isusumbong Kita, primetime series Diva, public affairs show Tonight with Arnold Clavio and Tunay Na Buhay, and The Ryzza Mae Show, among others. She was also part of the 50th-anniversary celebration of another Kapuso icon, German "Kuya Germs" Moreno, in 2013. We are honored to have been part of her life's journey and Ms. Elizabeth's legacy will forever remain in our hearts.

ABS-CBN Television Network, Inc.

Elizabeth Ramsey started out as a dreamer with undeniable talent and ambition. After ten years of trying to make it in the industry, she rose to fame and secured her biggest break in 1958 when she won the singing competition of "Student

Canteen," the first and biggest noontime variety program from the late 1950s to mid-1960s produced by ABS-CBN. - She was one of the great performers the network had produced when it was just starting out in television. Since then, the company had brought together amazing Filipino talents like her who conquered television and beyond and built their legacy in the industry. Five months before her death in 2015, she appeared on "Your Face Sounds Familiar" as a surprise guest. Her unforgettable stage presence reminded today's viewers of the comedy royalty's flair that did not wither over time. Elizabeth brought laughter to the show, a fitting curtain call to her five decades of contribution to Philippine entertainment. With a decades-long career marked by her quick wit, comedic talent and singing chops, she stood out among the rest and cemented her legacy as a revered Filipino music icon.

Susan Johnson: (Daughter and Author)

What can I say about my Mother? Well, everyone knew her as Ms. Elizabeth Ramsey, Mama Beth, Ate Beth, Ms. Ramsey, Mrs. Johnson, "Philippines' Queen of Rock N' Roll or "Queen of the Jungle," but for me, she was simply my "Ma!" I felt like the luckiest daughter in the world. She taught me everything in my life and been my mentor throughout my adulthood. She was not just my mother but also my best friend. She wanted me to be in showbiz since I was young and so I did. I remembered when I was an intern at St. Rita College as a first-year student in high school when she noticed that I didn't want to go back home anymore and wanted to live with the nuns. That's when she counseled me and said, "Are you kidding me! None of my kids will be a nun! You will be a dancer!" And guess what? She did make me one of her dancers in her show and took me out of St. Rita College for good. Another memorable moment, was when I woke up one morning and saw two families sleeping in our living room. I was puzzled because I didn't know these people and why they're sleeping in our living room. Lo' and behold, it was Ma that welcomed these families. This incident did not only happen once or twice but several times. She really had a heart of gold and compassion towards God's children. She wanted us, her children, Grandma Liling and Grandpa Doming to have everything in life, that's why she worked so hard to make that happen. She taught us how to love and be loved even though she herself never learned how to fall in love with any man. Ma and I enjoyed our company when she lived with me in the United States. Together we went shopping, clubbing, to church, movies, playing mahjong, casinos and most of all, cooking. I felt like her life was cut off too soon. I wanted her to read what I had written about her life. Most importantly, to spend more time with her and to hear more of her stories while laughing and crying out loud about it. Ma! I missed you so much! Ma! Thank you for your love, guidance, and support. May you rest in Peace!!! "I will always Love You, Ma!"

A TRUE TESTIMONY ABOUT HER FAITH

✝ There was a mailman who knew that my mother had a room in her house primarily designated as an altar just for her religious statues. One morning, he cordially asked my mother if he could bring his son to her. His son was diagnosed with brain cancer and not expected to live longer than a month or two. His last hope was a sign of a miracle that could cure his pain and suffering. My mother was saddened and quickly made him an appointment for both of them to schedule a prayer session at her altar. After he got off from work, he then brought his son and his wife at the house. When I saw the kid, I was shocked to see the holes all over his body including his scalp from a chemotherapy treatment. The kid was hardly walking and was supported by a cane while his father and mother were assisting him. My mother, the kid's mom and I proceeded to the altar to start praying the rosary while the kid and his father were left standing in the living room waiting to be called. After the first mystery, all of a sudden, the kid started to walk towards the altar with the help of his father. Standing at the door, he said, "I want to drink a glass of water." His father was so shocked because his son was no longer drinking any liquid through his mouth but through a solution that had been injected into his vein through an IV to replace lost fluids and to provide carbohydrates to his body. I then ran to the refrigerator to get him a glass of water. My mother and the kid's mother continued praying the rosary. After the kid drank the water, he proceeded to walk inside the altar. My mother then stood up from kneeling and touched all the wounds all over his body and head. My mother poured a little bit of holy water from Our Lady of Lourdes bottle in his glass and prayed over him. The kid finished drinking the glass of water and started walking towards the statues without his cane. We all wept uncontrollably because we were witnessing a miracle. The kid kept walking slowly until he regained more strength to kneel down and wept. We stopped reciting the rosary and just kneeled with him in a moment of silence. The kid then stood up on his own and told his parents "I will be okay!" We did not finish reciting the rosary because the kid wanted to go home and so they left. After several months, we never heard from them again until we had to move to another city. Years have gone by, and we never heard from that family again until one day, my mother and I were shopping at the mall when a man called out my mother's name "Ate Beth!" When she turned around, it was the father of that kid. He told us that after they left our house, his son started eating table food and drank lots of water. After weeks of chemotherapy treatment, the doctor told them that he was now cancer-free and he didn't have to finish the treatment. The doctor couldn't figure out how he got better so soon. The kid graduated high school, college, and his now a family man. He went back to our old house to deliver the good news and to thank my mother for praying for his son but we had moved.

✠ Unfortunately, whenever my mother went back to the Philippines, she always felt so all alone. Even though her nephews and nieces visited or lived with her, she still felt alone. To her, "Inday", her dog, was the only true companion she had in the Philippines. Her friends and family would come and go but Inday was always by her side. I do believe that house animals not only protect you but are also willing to give their lives to their master. When my mother was in the hospital in a coma, the doctor said that if she didn't wake up in two weeks, she would have 50-50 chance of survival. But a miracle happened; she woke up on the 14th day. On the same day and hour, my cousin, who was babysitting Inday found her helpless dead body under the dining table. This meant that Inday offered her own life so that my mother could live a little longer – "Inday, thank you for saving my mother's life and may you rest in peace!"

GRIEF OF HER PASSING

Ma had lived in the Philippines almost all her life; there were also long periods of time when she made her residency here in the U.S. but she always considered the Philippines home. I made it a point to visit her in the Philippines but when I was not able to go back, I would make sure I made it to wherever she was performing in the U.S. Even though we didn't see each other as often as we'd like, we talked several times a week; she would almost always catch me right when I was trying to get to bed. I don't think Ma ever got the time difference down, but it never bothered me. I just loved to hear her voice and we would sometimes talk for hours until I had to tell Ma I had to get ready for work.

One of the things we talked about often was how I wanted to see her more because she was getting older and I wanted us to spend as much time together as we could. Often times, our conversations would be about her coming to stay with me permanently. She had two shows booked here in the U.S. while she was staying with me. She always talked about how she wanted to play in Australia. After months of staying in the U.S., she needed to go back to the Philippines to check on her home. After a short period of time back in the Philippines, she received the good news that her chance to play in Australia would finally come to a fruition. She would be performing three solo shows in three different cities in Australia in November 2015. She was often requested to perform for the large Filipino community in Australia. The last time she visited Australia was in 1979.

In August 2015, her show contract agreement had been solidified. After all the excitement of finally getting a chance to perform solo in Australia, unfortunately, Mama's diabetes took a turn for the worse which resulted in her having to be hospitalized. One early morning, I received an abrupt call from my sister who lives in the Philippines that Mama had died from a heart attack. I started screaming and crying because I couldn't believe that it was true. It hadn't been that long since she was here with me. My sister who called only offered limited details and rushed me off the phone. I was given the name of the hospital where Mama had been admitted to, and I immediately contacted them to see if I could get more information regarding Mama's condition. My only objective was to speak to the doctor or the nurse who was overseeing Mama's medical status. To my surprise, the information that my sister had given to me earlier was false. The doctor stated that Mama's blood sugar level was so high that it caused her to fall into a state of deep unconsciousness which could be for an indefinite period of time. The doctor's prognosis was that she was in a comatose state and that the next two weeks would be critical to how she would recover from it. If her condition remained the same within two weeks, they would have to do more testing on other possibilities in reviving her before her whole body shut down which would lead her to be permanently paralyzed. For some insignificant reason, my sister posted on social media that "Elizabeth Ramsey had died from a heart attack." I was so furious reading the inaccurate news about her death, especially since it was posted by a family member. I told her to retract the false information that had been posted, and I took it upon myself to report the correct information.

In September 2015, I made all the preparations needed to take an emergency leave from my job, secure my home and contact our family members residing in the state of California to let them know about Mama's health condition, and not to believe any bogus information on social media. One of my cousins was my only contact because no other family member had any additional information about Ma's medical condition. As fast as I could, I booked the next available flight from San Francisco, California, to Manila International Airport.

As I had mentioned before, my sister in the Philippines, in her rush to judgment of Ma ever recovering, she called Ma's landlord and put in motion plans to terminate Ma's rental agreement since it was under her name. She took it upon herself to also instruct some of our relatives that were living with Ma to start packing out her house, but to her surprise, Ma got better. After three weeks of Ma being in the hospital, she finally discharged and sent home. With a strict warning from the doctor, she was instructed to pay more attention to her eating and medication regiments. My sister once again not anticipating Ma ever coming home, took her to her house because she did not want Ma to see what she had done to Ma's house. After several days, Ma demanded to go back to her own house because she always felt so uncomfortable, knowing that she had never been welcome in her daughter's home, and was loathed by my sister's husband. I talked to Ma briefly at the hospital and told her that I'm on my way to check on her.

When I arrived at Ma's house, I was shocked at how fragile she looked and the condition of her house. It broke my heart and literarily brought me to tears at how she was so frail and weak. Ma had always been a strong, little, outspoken firecracker, the one that was always in charge of everything. She's always been petite but this time, she was skin and bone weighing only 79 pounds. By just looking at her, I knew that she was not her old self. The illness had taken a toll on her, but I was still had high hopes that she would recover from this ordeal. Ma was a fighter and I knew if anyone could pull through this, it would be her. Ma's house was in such disarray and on top of all the mess, huge black rats were crawling everywhere, especially at night and when the house lights were off.

While I was staying in Ma's house, my cousins that were supposed to be taking care of her, told me that my sister had terminated my Ma's rental agreement and she would be forced to live with my sister and her family whom she didn't get along with and would never tolerate their ill-treatment. Ma loved to have her own space because of her religious statues and would not be allowed to display them as she pleased. My sister had converted from Catholicism and became a born-again Christian which she was not allowed to display religious statues or images inside their home. After Ma continued to refuse to move in with her, my sister then invited Ma and me to her home to talk about Ma's situation. I told her that I had contacted several of my friends in the U.S., also family and friends in the Philippines to help me search for another house to rent and store her belongings except for the religious statues and images. One of the major topics of conversation at my sisters began with, *"Why was the house infested with all kinds of crawling creatures? How could you even let this happen to our mother? You only live two minutes away from her and you never bothered to check on her?"* I was really disappointed in her response. I understood that she also has her own family responsibilities but to disregard your mother was not the right thing to do. To my sister's credit, she did help our mother financially for a while. My cousins, Ma and I did find some houses, and some family friends even offered their property. But unfortunately, Ma was not thrilled about the choices. A week after I arrived, Ma then asked me to finish recording her life-long story events because she felt that she may not make it much longer. I wanted to take her back with me to the U.S. but because of her health, she was not allowed to travel long distance. Regrettably, I had a limited amount of time before I had to leave Ma in the care of my cousins and my sister. On the day of my departure, I had a heart to heart talk with Ma, *"Ma! Ka on gyud perme para mu kusug ka usab. Gusto nako na pag balik nako mag-uban nata. Mangayo ko ug usab na adlaw sa akong trabaho sa pagbalik nako usab para maayo ang imong mga gamit. Para mag uban na ta permanente sa America."* (Ma! Please eat so you would be strong again. I want us to be together again. I am going to ask my employer to give me more days off so we could make arrangements for your belongings. Then you would live permanently in America with me.) Sadly, after I left that day. I received a phone call from my cousin that Ma was back in the hospital and this time her health condition did not look like she would pull through.

On October 8, 2015, at 7 PM, after two weeks of being back home in California, I was in the middle of a choir rehearsal at St. James the Apostles church in Fremont, preparing to celebrate our Wednesday's normal adoration to Our Mother of Perpetual Help Novena at 7:30 PM. Normally, I would turn off my cell phone while rehearsing but why did I forget to turn it off this time? It seemed like a premonition that something would happen. I was so stunned when my phone rang because I thought I had turned it off. When the phone rang, my heart started beating fast for no apparent reason. When I answered the phone call, it was the saddest moment of my life which still haunts me to this day. It was from my sister in the Philippines notifying me that Mama had just passed away. My heartbeat got faster and my whole body just felt so numb that I froze. Then all of a sudden, my tears started pouring out uncontrollably and I screamed so loud - so loud that I was hoping God would hear me and tell me that the news was not true, that my loving mother was dead. I couldn't stop saying "No! No! No! This is not true, Mama promised to wait for me because I was planning to go back home to the Philippines. She promised me that she would get better and be strong again. Mahal Na Santo Niño said she would live to be a hundred years old. This is not true! This is not true!" I kept crying and screaming at the top of my lungs asking God to give me a different message. While my sister from the Philippines listened to my sobbing and screaming, she decided to hang-up the phone. I kept saying, "Hello?! Hello?!" But no response. I then realized that she definitely hung up the phone on me. I continued sobbing and screaming while some of the choir members were comforting me and praying for me to accept what had just happened. When I was finally able to accept the fact that Mama was gone and had joined God in heaven, I joined the choir members including the congregation to pray for my mother's soul, and for God to open the gate of heaven to welcome her. Father Antony Vazhappily was so kind to extend the novena's blessings dedicated to my mother. I was not able to finish the novena because I couldn't stop crying. When I was able to regroup myself, I started calling back my sister in the Philippines to coordinate the funeral arrangements, but sadly she did not answer her phone or return my calls. I texted her but only ended up having a back and forth confrontation with her husband. I stopped entertaining that situation and decided to contact my sister's former show manager to see if she could be kind enough to call my sister so we could have a family conference call including Mary Ann and Isaac, my siblings here in the US. She, in turn, said that my sister had already made the funeral arrangements and we didn't need to come to the Philippines, because my sister had already made plans to have our mother cremated the following week, on a Monday morning. My God! My God! Why is she doing this? I knew that she had animosity against mama but she went too far by excluding her sisters and brother and denying our mother's wish to be buried. I proceeded right away to purchase round-trip tickets for Mary Ann, Isaac and myself.

Since Mary Ann and I are from the Bay Area of California, our flights were scheduled to arrive on Sunday, while Isaac's flight was scheduled to arrive on Saturday because he would be flying out from Los Angeles, California. My cousin, Hermie, and his kids were kind enough to pick us up from the Manila Ninoy Aquino International Airport. We directly headed to St. Peter Memorial Chapel at Quezon City. There I saw my beautiful, loving mother's helpless body lying in a casket. I started crying, talking to myself and saying, "Ma, why did you leave us so soon? I will definitely make sure that your wish will be granted. I promised you! You will be buried, not cremated! One of these days, I want your body to be examined. Before I left you from my last visit, you were doing fine and I was looking forward to your recovery. I'm going to hire a forensic pathologist to examine your body to find out the real cause of your death." I then sensed that everyone in our family, including Isaac, was already convinced by my sister in the Philippines to go along with her wishes. My sister was so shocked to see that Mary Ann and especially me had made it at the funeral home. Now the showdown started: I let my sister in the Philippines deliver her twenty-minute speech about letting Mama go, to follow the white light, telling our mother not to suffer anymore, and just let herself go. She already bought a cremation plot a year ago for mama and so the final decision would be for her body to be cremated. This is when I stood up and told her it is my turn to talk: "First of all, I would like to ask you why you did not return any of my calls, text, email? Why did you eagerly make the funeral arrangements without consulting your sisters and brother? You told everyone that you solely paid for all hospital bills which was a lie? What happened to the $1,000.00 dollars I sent you to help pay for the hospital bills? Actually, someone told me that there were lots of people that donated money to help you pay the hospital bills and expenses. Besides the individual donations, television networks had pitched in by also helping to pay for Ma's hospital bills, funeral service, and media coverage. Why would you lie about Mama only having one child that took care of her? I can go on and on about these, but the one that really bothered me was someone that was not even a blood relative had the audacity to text me that you are the only Ramsey because Isaac, Mary Ann and I's last name is Johnson. Have you forgotten that mama's married last name is Johnson, and Ramsey is her single last name so that made it our middle name? Let me tell you right to your face! Mama will not be cremated! God will find a way for mama to be buried." The confrontation heated up and eventually got interrupted when she started to scream saying: *"Tama na! Tama na!"* (Enough! Enough!). She then ran off towards mama's casket. That wish to bury Mama became the subject of the turmoil at mama's funeral. To break out from the chaotic situation, Mary Ann and I were given a ride to look for a possible grave site where we could purchase a plot. Unfortunately, it was late Sunday afternoon, and most of the cemeteries were already closed. We only saw one, but it was so dirty that there was no way mama could be buried there. We went back to the funeral home dismayed because I was not sure how I could properly bury our mother. While I was secluding myself from everyone to pray for God's blessings, some family members sat with me trying to convince me to accept my sister in the Philippines request to cremate our mother so there could be peace in our family. But my heart and soul would not allow this to happen so I told them to leave me alone. After the presided Holy Mass, I slowly walked toward my mother's casket and whispered to her as if she was alive. I told her, "Ma, it is only Mary Ann and I who were the only people championing for your burial. Ma! Please help us to make your wish come true. Ma! Please you have to show me a miracle by sending someone who can help us. Everyone is ganging on me and Mary Ann and we are running out of time. Tomorrow morning, your body has been scheduled to be cremated and the majority of the family desire for you to be cremated." All of a sudden, when I turned around, I saw Mama's closest friends and also family friends: Rose Uy and Gina Tria. They were sisters that were very devoted to Santo Niño. Rose and Gina came behind me and started crying on my shoulders. Then Gina whispered in my ear and said, "Why Mama Beth is going to be cremated when she told all of us, even on TV, that if she ever passed away, she wants to be buried? I need to speak with you." My eyes just literary lit up and I was so surprised at how she knew what I had been praying to Mama about. We parted and sat outside the funeral to have a private moment. Before I could open my mouth, she quickly spoke and said, "We are here to talk to you because, as you know, your sister in the Philippines and our family are not on good terms. What we are ready to propose will not be heard by your sister. You are the only one that we can tell our proposal. We would like to offer you one of our family vacant plots to bury Mama temporarily until you we will be able to buy her own plot. You have five years to make the final preparations to where you want her to permanently be put to rest. She will never rest in peace if we are not going to honor her wishes. We will help you pay for any extra expenses just to make this happen." I was so stunned that all I could say was, "Thank you Lord and thank you both!" And then, I told them, "Mama sent you here to help me and now I know she heard my plea. Let's go back inside and talk to Mama so I can tell her 'Ma! Thank you and I love you'" We then proceeded to the funeral home's office to speak with the evening manager to make new arrangements that there would be no more cremation and Mama would be buried at the Holy Garden Cemetery at Antipolo City. I went back upstairs to deliver the good news to everyone that Mama would be buried tomorrow at the Holy Garden Cemetery and explained to them the sudden miracle. My family members and friends' faces were so surprised and in disbelief; how could this happen at the last minute? They were so worried on how my sister in the Philippines would accept this so-called good news. They told me that my sister and her husband had just left. So, I quickly texted my sister the good news and told her we were now at the funeral home's office talking to the night manager, making new burial arrangements. I specifically told the night manager not to remove Mama's body because we were going to have a family meeting first thing tomorrow morning. I felt like I was walking on cloud nine and Mary Ann was also so happy. The sisters (Gina & Rose) then drove us to our hotel.

Because of the good news, I could not sleep well. I tossed and turned waiting for the morning dawn to come, so we could have our family meeting to give Mama her final resting place. The sisters picked up Mary Ann and me from the hotel around 7 AM so we could be early enough to be there before everyone else arrived. We arrived at the St. Peter Funeral Home around 8:30 AM and went straight to the manager's office. To our surprise, we were greeted by the manager to tell us that there was no need to go upstairs because my sister and some of our family members came even earlier and ordered the funeral home to remove your Mama's body and send it to St. Peter's Crematorium to be cremated. They had just left ten minutes before we arrived. I started screaming uncontrollably and was so much disbelief on what I just heard. I then told the manager; "Look! You better do something! I told you guys last night not to remove our mother's body without our consent. You violated our request so you better call the Crematorium to stop the process now, or I will sue your company for violating our request! Do you understand? Do something now! You don't have to get your security to hold me down; all I want is for you to make that emergency phone call to put a hold on everything!" She finally got hold of the Crematorium's office and ordered to halt everything, because we were on our way. Suddenly, the sisters, Mary Ann, and I left heading quickly to St. Peter's Crematorium. On the way, I texted my sister, asking her, "Why did you order Mama's body to be removed?" She replied, "You can now have Mama's body and do what you want with it!" I felt so relieved that she finally agreed to Mama's request. When we arrived at St. Peter's Crematorium, the attendant escorted Mary Ann and me to an office. There sat my sister, Isaac and a stranger who I thought would be the pastor to bless Mama's body, because of my sister's religion. As soon as Mary Ann and I sat down, the stranger proceeded to introduce himself as a lawyer who was hired to mediate our situation. Then my sister got up and forcefully told us, "I know why both of you are here!" Then she looked at Isaac, and said to him, "You know what to do, and you know what to say!" Then she stormed out of the room. Mary Ann and I looked at each other, wondering what was going on here. The lawyer then proceeded to tell us of a by law in the Philippines that when siblings could not make the final decision on how to bury the deceased, the eldest child would be the final decision maker, which in this case, it would be Isaac.

He then asked Isaac, "Mr. Johnson, what will be your final decision?" Isaac crossed his arms and then looked into his eyes and said, "Cremation!" I then screamed "No!" and Mary Ann said, "We are going to get our own lawyer!" Then Isaac, like my sister, stormed out of the room as well. I then told the lawyer, "Look! You cannot honor his words because he has been manipulated and been paid off. Under the law, you cannot honor someone's words when he is under the influence of drugs." The lawyer then said, "Please calm down Ms. Johnson because I did not know about Isaac's addiction. I will get back to you after I negotiated with them. Please step outside for awhile to get some fresh air and have a bottle of water." The security guard escorted Mary Ann and I outside, where we started praying the rosary, hoping for this drama to be over soon for Mama's sake. After long hours of discussion, my sister and Isaac finally agreed to release Mama's body under Mary Ann and my supervision. My sister then asked for a refund of the advance payment to release Mama's body. Ms. Gina's friend, in turn, was kind enough to pay for the release of Mama's body for burial. After all of this turmoil, we finally had Mama's body carried into a funeral car to be transported to Holy Garden Cemetery. On October 13, 2015, Mama was finally put to rest temporarily. Mama was celebrated by some of our family members and closest friends except my sister, Isaac and other family members who were championing my sister's side.

On October 8th, 2016, I was granted from Antipolo City an exhumation of Mama's body. A special thank you to San Carlos City, Negros Occidental City Mayor, Mr. Gerardo Valmayor, who granted my request to provide a truck to transport Mama's coffin from Bacolod City to San Carlos City. Now, Mama is permanently laid to rest surrounded by her brother, Federico, Grandma Liling, and, Grandpa Arturo.

"She is finally back home"

EULOGY

ELIZABETH RAMSEY
QUEEN OF PHILIPPINE ROCK N' ROLL

On October 8, 2015, I lost my mother and my best friend. Her diabetes became unmanageable when she turned 83 years of age. She succumbed to severe sepsis and diabetes mellitus – type 2, seizure disorder and she died due to multi-organ failure. I will miss her presence, beautiful smile, and humor for the rest of my life. Words can't express how much she meant to me and our family. I think we all remembered Ms. Elizabeth Ramsey from her live show performances, fascinating acting abilities, non-scripted comedy, having an extravagant altar, loving and compassionate welfare for those in need, beautiful inside and out, but her most special attribute is being our Mother. She had the gift of gab and somehow was able to have a complete stranger share their life story with her within their very first conversations – she truly had a sensitive and compassionate heart. Vice-versa, she would look at someone and start telling them what's going on in their lives and then predict what the future has in store for them – she truly also had a gift of what we call a "Third Eye." As one of her children, she taught us to have strong values and the importance of family, faith, hard work, kindness, tolerance, generosity, forgiveness, and love. She had that very strong presence that makes anyone tell the truth. She was also a stubborn, gentle but direct and had an amazing sense of humor.

Some of the most important things in her life were:

Santo Niño and Blessed Mother – Every home base she had, there is always a room designated for her altar. The visual expression of her Catholic faith was expressed through her collections of different statues of Saints. But her special devotion was to Santo Niño which she collected over 200 images in her entire life. She believed that Santo Niño has guided her since childhood. Her testimony is that "If you were born Catholic, then you die Catholic." What she was trying to convey is that "If it's not broken, then don't fix it!" Unfortunately, after her death, some of the Philippine images were dispersed to unknown sources.

Family – She managed to raise her four children as a single Mother through the only thing she knew, the entertainment industry. Mama said that we could be whatever we wanted to be as long as you always respect others. When we were growing up, my mother made sure my siblings and I were always taken care of. She supported her children including her Mother, her Brother and his family and other family members who needed help. She would sacrifice her own happiness for ours and there was no age limit when it came to supporting her children finances or personal issues. She was one of those mothers who you could depend on. She always had your back and gave you the best advice under any circumstances. As a Grandmother, I had to admit that she was not the most civilized language educator to little children. In her younger years, she would curse like a sailor. For example; We lived together at one time, so she babysat my children for a while when I was working. One day, I received a phone call from my son's teacher. She said that my son Rodney had a confrontation with his classmate and he said some words in a different language which we did not understand. So, when I talked to Rodney, I asked him: "Rodney, what did you say to the other kid?" Rodney replied: Grandma taught me that when someone wants to fight with me to say the word "Anak nang Puta! (Son of a bitch!)." All I can do is shake my head. Yeah! That's Grandma alright!

Friends – As a friend, she was the most loyal and truthful friend you could have. She would be in your face and be frank about it. I know that she was not the easiest person to deal with sometimes but she would always have her reasons. You really have to understand where she was coming from. One time she told one of her friends, "Day! Sige kainin mo yong doughnut araw-araw, maging kasing laki yong puet mo sa butas nang doughnut. (Girl! Keep eating that doughnut every day and your ass will be as big as the doughnut hole." Her friend was offended for awhile but Mama was right. Her friend became diabetic and her legs almost got amputated. In spite of that offensive comment, overall, she thanked, Mama because she started to watch her diet, loss some weight and eventually got rid of diabetes. Mama believed that tough love and honesty is the best quality of a true friend.

Neighbors - When we were younger we didn't understand her generosity. Often, she would open her home to families who were in need of shelter. She also loved to cook, so she fed those who were hungry. She would give anyone the shirt off her back and go out of her way to help a friend or strangers in need. She was not a person that brags every time she helped someone. She instilled in her heart of what Jesus said: "What you do to the least of my people, you do it unto me," and so she did.

Ms. Ramsey, Mama Beth, Ate Beth, Tita Beth or whatever you want to call her, she was all of that. One of the most famous names that she was called that became her trademark was: "Queen of the Jungle!" Mama was the "Rock!" of my heart "N' Roll!" of my soul. For, she was a fighter and her incredible tenacity had shown up in her strong will to live with that terrible disease. When I looked at her before she was buried, I saw a beautiful face at peace that had transitioned out of this world and into the next. I hope she was happy to see her loved ones who went before her. She will be definitely missed by not only her children but everyone. Ma was the light of my life as I am sure she was the light in all of yours. I know she would be watching over us and she would stay with us in spirit. Let us remember Ms. Ramsey, as the carefree and loving person she was. Our families thank you for celebrating the life of a great fabulous woman as we honor her memory.

ELIZABETH RAMSEY
Philippines Legend and will never be forgotten!

Elizabeth Ramsey
1931 - 2015

"I LOVE YOU MA! WE WILL ALWAYS BE!"

Sansu Ramsey
About the Author

Every one of us has a story, but when my mother, Elizabeth, wanted me to share her colorful life experiences with you, I had no choice but to honor her wishes. I started this journey of writing Ma's book with her five years ago to give her fans and supporters a chance to know her personally beginning from her young life throughout her amazing entertainment career. She would always tell me, "To follow your dreams, and don't let anyone stop you from accomplishing anything you want, in spite of any obstacles that may come your way." I am the third child of Ma, Beth, who was born in Pasay City, Manila, but raised in San Carlos City, Negros Occidental by my Grandma Liling and Lolo Doming. Being the darkest of all Ramsey's, besides my Grandfather, Mr. Ramsey, I was harshly discriminated, viciously ridiculed, by the locals. In the early 60's, as a dark black girl, you would be considered the ugliest person. I literally hid in the closet, so no one would call me names, and that's why I developed an inferiority complex. Thank God! That I had a mother, like Elizabeth, that believed and protected me. She encouraged me at a young age by introducing me to showbusiness, which taught me to be proud of who I am. I hope you will enjoy reading my mom's gripping, surprising, very candid, and fascinating story of her life's adventure.

Thank you so much and God bless you always!
Love! Peace! & Joy!

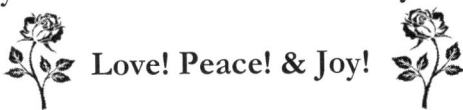

Made in the USA
Middletown, DE
29 November 2023